Marine Policy

Marine Policy

A Comparative Approach

John King Gamble, Jr.
The Pennsylvania State University

With

Daniel B. Charter, Jr.
Charles I. Cook
Charlene Quinn Dunn
Maria Kazanowska
Christopher B. Llana
Edwin F. Stein, Jr.

Studies in Marine Affairs

Lexington Books
D.C. Heath and Company
Lexington, Massachusetts
Toronto

Library of Congress Cataloging in Publication Data

Gamble, John King.
   Marine policy.

   Includes index.
   1. Marine resources and state. I. Title
GC1017.G34   333.9'164   76-13931   ISBN 0-669-00728-5

Published simultaneously in Canada

Printed in the United States of America

International Standard Book Number: 0-669-00728-5

Library of Congress Catalog Card Number: 76-13931

To Clare

Contents

List of Figures

List of Tables

Acknowledgments

Graduate students at the University of Rhode Island enrolled in Political Science 578 have made a significant contribution to this work. They confirmed my suspicion that there was something to the comparative study of marine policy. Additionally, they proved to be excellent critics as some of the ideas contained herein were being developed. Some of these students prepared studies of individual states' marine policies, some of which form the basis for chapter 2 of this work.

I owe a debt of gratitude to Professor Robert L. Friedheim who nurtured my interest in marine policy and provided assistance in data collection and analysis. The encouragement and counsel of Professor Friedheim was invaluable.

My wife, Clare, played a pivotal role in the preparation of the final manuscript. Her help with many important details made the whole undertaking go much more smoothly than otherwise would have been possible.

Marine Policy

1 Introduction

Man's reliance on the oceans is hardly a new phenomenon. At least since recorded history, the oceans have been used as a source of protein as well as for commercial and strategic navigation. Nevertheless, the twentieth century has seen substantial changes in the intensity and kinds of ocean uses. Although the changes occurring in many use areas, for example, fishing and navigation, may seem merely quantitative, it may be that the Hegelian nodal line has been crossed, that is, quantitative change has, in fact, become qualitative.[1] For example, it is projected that by 1980 total worldwide merchant-fleet capacity will increase from 112 to more than 800 million deadweight tons.[2] In the area of fisheries, change is less spectacular. Total world fish catch in 1972 was estimated at 55.8 million metric tons, a figure that can be expected to increase only slightly unless significant changes occur in the types of species harvested.[3]

Among the more recent uses to which the oceans have been put is the exploitation of minerals, especially petroleum and natural gas. At present slightly more than 25 percent of all petroleum comes from off-shore wells.[4] This percentage will increase substantially in the near future. Furthermore, oil exploration is taking place at greatly increased depths. In 1973 almost all oil exploration was at depths of 600 feet or less; technology has improved so rapidly that this 600-foot limit will soon be extended to 2,000 feet.[5]

Greatly increased technological sophistication has created the possibility of exploiting minerals (manganese nodules) from the deep ocean floor. Although considerable investment will be needed to mine these minerals usually found at depths of 730 to 5,800 meters,[6] one study has estimated that tax revenues from nodule mining will be in the $50 to $150 million range by 1985.[7]

Numerous other statistics could be cited, but these suffice to make a basic point, that is, resources and uses of the oceans will play an increasingly important role. Ocean resources will be expected to contribute to the resolution of problems created by scarcities in many areas including protein and energy. This means that the decisions countries make about the oceans and ocean resources will assume an unparalleled level of urgency.

In the pages that follow, I develop a systematic approach toward national postures about the oceans. This analysis must begin with a careful appraisal and definition of marine policy, a term that is used frequently, usually without precision, let alone explicit definition. Once the definitions and groundwork have been laid, the marine policies of five countries are examined in somewhat greater detail. The third section broadens the focus to the entire world by

1

applying a model to the marine policies of each country in the world. This model provides a way to look for patterns of interrelationship among some 90 national characteristics. This two-pronged approach is designed to provide a satisfactory compromise between the necessity of accommodating the idiosyncrasies of individual countries in order to appreciate their marine policies and the desirability of searching for patterns and consistency among the largest possible sample of countries. Obviously, the most desirable solution, detailed analyses for each state in the world, would be impractical.

Public Policy and Marine Policy

There seems to be an assumption in much of the literature that marine policy is a broad, self-defining phenomenon somehow derived from countries' attempts to maximize their benefits from hydrospace. For the purposes of this inquiry, it is necessary to add considerable specificity to the concept of marine policy. One approach to this problem is to examine public policy about which a more systematic and theoretical literature has been developed and attempt to apply the findings to the national marine policies of countries. The validity of this strategy rests on the assumption that marine policy is a subset of national public policies.

There are several workable definitions of public policy that apply directly to the marine area. Richard Hofferbert suggests that *public policy* is "purposive action taken for or to the public."[8] Such a definition is broad enough to encompass actions taken by public authorities as well as any other actions taken that affect the public.[9] This is advantageous when applied to the marine area, where nongovernmental actions can be very important. A somewhat more abstract approach to public policy would define policy as the relationship between governments and their environments.[10] Such a definition could be applied easily to marine policy by limiting it to those environments having some relationship to the oceans. It has also been suggested that studies and analyses of public policies are distinguished by their focus on authoritative rules.[11] Such a formulation, however, requires a definition of exactly what constitutes an authoritative rule.

In a somewhat similar vein, Philip Gregg defines public-policy analysis as the systematic study of rules.[12] However, the use of the word "rules" connotes a narrow definition of policy, one that would be restricted principally to formal legislative and executive actions. Although aimed primarily at foreign policy, Bernard Cohen and Scott Harris provide an interesting definition of policy:

. . . it is a set of goals, directives, or intentions, formulated by persons in official or authoritative positions, directed at some actor or condition in the environment beyond the sovereign nation state.[13]

This could be easily modified to fit marine or oceans policy.

Regardless of what specific definition of public policy is accepted, there are several recurring rules or admonitions that should be followed in trying to analyze public policy. A common theme seems to be that analyses of public policy tend to be too simplistic and focused on too narrow a set of indicators. It is necessary to consider the mechanisms by which public policy is set in addition to the actual policy outcomes.[14] Policy analysis must provide "a theoretical framework [that is] more than just categories. It must enable us to decompose rule-ordered processes into comparable units of analysis."[15] Frequently there is an inherent conflict between two approaches to policy analysis, one macro and the other micro. Macro policy analysis usually adopts a broad systems-analysis posture, whereas micro analysis concentrates on elements like the organizational development of the authoritative body.[16] Both of these approaches, each with strong advocates, find that the other approach asks the wrong questions and proceeds in the wrong way.[17] These approaches have been termed narrow and broad views of policy—narrow approaches include statutes and executive orders, and the broad approach concerns itself with goals and general patterns of decisions.[18]

Policy analysis must be careful not to limit itself to official protestations of policy. This stems in part from the fact that a "policy need not be declared to be a policy . . . analysis cannot rely on manifest statements."[19] Many feel it is insufficient to examine only policy outputs or only policy process as has often been done; both must be examined to get at the heart of policy.[20] David Easton in what has become a political science classic warns that one must distinguish between policy outputs and outcomes.[21] *Policy outputs* are simply the authoritative allocation of values of society, whereas *outcomes* are the ultimate consequences of that policy for society.[22]

Definitions and Approaches to Marine Policy

Unfortunately, the problem of defining marine policy has seldom been addressed in a systematic, rigorous way. In fact, many works that have included the terms "marine policy" or "ocean policy" in their titles make no effort to define the exact nature and limits of the concept. Although it may be sufficient for political rhetoric to leave the term as nebulous as possible, it is essential to this inquiry to establish a firm definition of marine policy. Although the exact nature of such a definition is arguable, at least it can be applied with consistency and uniformity.

There is a reluctance to adhere to a concrete, precise definition of marine policy. This difficulty has been attributed to the diverse number of public and private interests involved in the policy making.[23] Such diversity is unquestionable, but it is not sufficient reason to avoid definition. Quite the contrary, the large number of actors and interests represented may create more need for definitional precision.

In an interesting analysis of Canadian marine policy, Barry Buzan and Barbara Johnston view marine policy as political goals that can take the form of no action, or of unilateral, bilateral, regional, or global action.[24] There are at least several major elements to any marine policy. It has been suggested that these be trifurcated into security, economic, and political concerns.[25] Many people have suggested that marine policy can be viewed as a resolution of two opposing forces, one representing coastal-economic interests and the other military-strategic interests.[26] Others would modify this formulation only slightly emphasizing coastal versus maritime interests.[27] This approach resembles the inclusive-exclusive claims approach championed by Myres McDougal and William Burke among others:

The most basic goals for which the process is maintained embrace of course all common interests, but a strong presumption is established in favor of inclusive interest, and exclusive interest is protected only when its protection will clearly contribute to the common good.[28]

Of course in the 15 years since McDougal and Burke completed their work, we have seen a precipitous shift in favor of exclusive claims; in this process the "common good" of which McDougal and Burke wrote is not nearly so simple as once thought.

It has also been recognized that there remains considerable subjectivity about which particular elements one chooses to emphasize in any analysis of marine policy.[29] For example, ocean policy issues transcend the traditional boundaries between foreign and domestic policy.[30] Ocean policy has been termed a loose policy system, that is, there are a number of weak interrelationships on subissues.[31] This creates the possibility of a myriad of different marine policy stands by different countries, some of which may contain apparent inconsistencies precisely because of the looseness of the policy system.

It may be helpful in coming to grips with a definition of marine policy to relate that policy to other types of policy that may have been studied in a more systematic way. There are obvious ties between marine policy and foreign policy. Both types of national policy give a high priority to security interests, in fact marine policy may have brought about a greatly expanded concept of national security at least in the case of the United States.[32] One problem with the comparison to foreign policy is that it tends to emphasize only the maritime component of marine policy largely ignoring resource-coastal aspects of that policy. This deficiency becomes all the more pronounced when one considers that, for the vast majority of the states in the world, maritime concerns play little *direct* role in marine policy. Most developing states are little concerned with the movement of commercial vessels, let alone military vessels. Thus it appears that acceptance of too direct a parallel between foreign and marine policy may be inappropriate, especially in the case of the numerous developing countries, which because of their numerical preponderance must be adequately accommodated in any definition.

In marine affairs as in all specialized subject areas, practitioners tend to bemoan the lack of attention they receive from the highest levels of government. Marine policy, in spite of the protestations of certain bureaucrats in Washington, Paris, Delhi, Moscow, and so on, is not and never will be the quintessence of all national policies. This is not to imply that marine policy is unimportant, merely that the importance must be placed in some kind of reasonable perspective. Marine policy must compete with other policy loci for the attention of government leaders. It is perfectly reasonable that many in the ocean-policy area may feel ignored by those possessing real power.[33] As Davis Bobrow aptly commented, ocean policy "will be strongly affected by busy, important people with no professional commitment to ocean policy."[34] Additionally, there seems to be the feeling among practitioners that ocean policy must strive to maintain a separate identity. A workshop convened to study the subject of ocean policy research felt that ocean policy problems were better not treated as mere extensions of land problems.[35] However, there is a distinct possibility that those who advocate a separate identity for ocean policy may be taking a position that is operationally untenable, since marine elements are contained in many different aspects of public policy. Energies might be better directed at identifying policy linkages rather than advocating separate treatment.

Although marine policy has certain special characteristics, it is difficult, if not impossible, to treat it in isolation from other national policies. This is evident in the United States' situation in which marine policy has been closely related to foreign policy, security policy, and more recently to resource policy. Although there are certainly unique aspects to marine policy, it would seem futile to examine it in a vacuum. Any marine policy is shaped by many factors having little to do with explicit marine characteristics. These external forces can be both procedural and substantive. Buzan and Johnson express the effect of procedure in very interesting terms:

Does policy [in the sense of national political goals] predetermine the outcome of multilateral political negotiations on the law of the sea? Or, instead, do the game [ocean politics] and its rules [multilateral bargaining on a wide range of issues] create their own requirements and lead the players into goals they never intended?[36]

This points out an important aspect of marine policy—it may be distorted and shaped in ways that are not intrinsically logical given the set of preconditioning national characteristics. There is also the very real possibility that certain non-marine factors (substantive factors) may be so important to a country that they influence (distort) marine policy so it bears little resemblance to the policy one might otherwise have expected.

Marine Policy: A Suggested Definition and Strategy

It seems that the safest, that is, the least refutable, definition of *marine policy* is simply the relationship between government and the ocean environment. However, a somewhat more workable approach is to modify the formulation of Cohen and Harris—marine policy is a set of goals, directives, and intentions formulated by authoritative persons and having some relation to the marine environment. This will be accepted as the working definition for the balance of this study. Even such a broad definition has problems. One wonders what real relationship exists between goals and intentions on the one hand and marine policy on the other, especially since such things often fall into the platitudinous abyss of political rhetoric. For example, it is difficult to think of a single state whose government has not officially advocated full use of the marine resources and control of marine pollution so that future generations can enjoy fully the benefits of the oceans. If such protestations are not accompanied by concrete government action, are they really a part of marine policy? It might well be that such lip-service statements have some cumulative effect, that is, if they are repeated often enough, they tend to result in actual governmental action. Conversely one might argue, somewhat cynically, that goals and intentions actually may be counterproductive to the ends that they advocate. General statements about desirable policy goals may be a vehicle to placate those interests advocating change and more concrete policy. If this is the case, they are not policy in the real sense of the word. For obvious reasons it is preferable to concentrate on actual governmental actions rather than having to make difficult judgments about whether a certain statement by a government leader, not buttressed by implementary action, actually constitutes marine policy.

There is no paucity of things that do actually constitute marine policy. Instead the problem is finding a manageable list of items that give some indication of the diversity and complexity of marine policy. The characteristics chosen must have relevance for a large percentage of states, since a principal purpose of this study is gaining a truly global perspective on marine policy. It is also important that indicators of marine policy not be treated completely in isolation. It is reasonable to assume that certain other characteristics, some of which are geographic, some nonmarine, may dispose countries towards certain types of marine policy. For example, one would presume that the amount of fishing resources near a state's coast would influence the development of a fishing fleet by that state. Obviously, some states have developed large fishing fleets principally to fish in international or foreign waters. But one would nevertheless expect a relationship between coastal resources and the policy decision to develop an extensive fishery. Carrying this example further, one might expect that the policy decision to engage in distant water fishing might result from an unusual set of national characteristics, such as the unavailability of land-based protein sources.

The approach adopted here views marine policy in terms of an input-output model. The assumptions upon which such a model is based are straightforward. It is assumed that a group of input characteristics sets the bases and directions of most aspects of marine policy. For the purposes of this inquiry *inputs* are defined as objective, quantifiable characteristics from which policy can be developed. Note that this definition is relatively narrow, excluding everything done by man. This formulation is somewhat arbitrary since the actual boundaries of states were, of course, determined by people. But for the sake of consistency, the current geographic boundaries of each independent state in the world have been taken as given; inputs then are those attributes or characteristics deriving from the basic geographic situation. Inputs include both marine and nonmarine characteristics, for example, shoreline length, seabed area, land area, offshore oil reserves, and so on.

Policy is created when states (or entities within states) make decisions about using marine resources. The way policy is made is termed *processing* in the model. This is where the inputs are transformed into actual policy. It is, of course, very difficult to go into detail about the actual "processing" that takes place in each state. Because the processing section molds, modifies, shapes, and distorts the inputs, it can be viewed in terms of a filter. The individual state studies contained in chapter 2 will focus on the processing characteristics of the countries involved. For the purposes of the general policy model contained in chapter 3, the processing section is largely ignored. This is for obvious reasons. The processing section contains, among other elements, the value system within which the country operates, the bureaucratic structure by which policy is set and implemented, and the decision-making processes used in the country. Although these and similar elements of the processing section of the model are vitally important, they are difficult, if not impossible, to specify in a precise, systematic way for each country. Value systems simply cannot be reduced to a single number the way one might handle fish catch.

Outputs in the model consist of those things usually thought of as elements of public policy. In general these are any country actions produced by the actions and decisional choices of people and governments. Of course there is considerable variation in things included in the output side of the model. Output characteristics range from population to seaborne trade, to status vis-à-vis marine treaties, to current production of certain minerals. The outputs were selected to indicate relevant aspects of states' public policies in general as well as marine policy in particular. The complete model consists of nearly 90 variables, each of which is explained in detail in chapter 7. The model is illustrated in figure 1-1.

To reiterate, marine policy is the set of goals, directives, and intentions formulated by authoritative persons and having some relationship to the marine

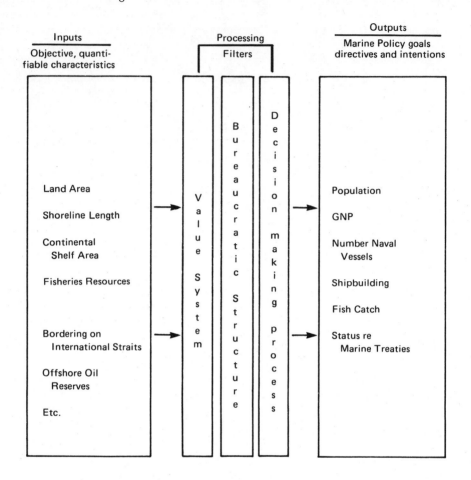

Figure 1-1. Model of Marine Policy Making

environment. Marine policy is thought of as a subset of public policy and, to be fully understood, it must be related to other aspects of public policy as well as to fundamental national characteristics, that is, the inputs. The analysis of marine policy proceeds on two fronts. First, detailed examinations of five states' policies are made. Then, the focus is broadened to include every independent state with a concomitant loss of detail and diminished understanding of the idiosyncrasies of individual countries.

2 Marine Policy: Five Specific Cases

In this chapter the model of marine policy is applied to five specific country situations. Special concern is paid to the processing section of the model, since these elements are largely neglected in chapter 3 which tries to accommodate all states. The selection of the five states analyzed here is somewhat arbitrary. But the five—Canada, Nigeria, Iran, the Philippines, and the Peoples' Republic of China—do provide wide variety in terms of geography, marine orientation, and ideology. It was felt that certain countries have already been the subject of detailed analysis. Thus, these five provide range, diversity, and in most instances have not been extensively studied before.

The Case of Canada

Background

Marine activities have traditionally played a very important role in the development of Canada. With one of the longest coastlines in the world, bordering on three oceans, it is only natural that the sea would play a prominent role in the history, economy, and philosophy of the nation.

Permanent European influences were not felt in Canada until the end of the fifteenth century. In 1497, only five years after Columbus made his initial voyage, John Cabot, commissioned by the King of England, sailed to the new world in the *Mathew*. He was searching for a route to China when he landed in the Newfoundland area and claimed the region for England. Cabot's report initiated the first industry of the new world indicating that fish were so plentiful they were able to bring in loads of cod merely by casting a basket into the water. The first distant water fishing-fleet activity off North America began almost five centuries ago.

Inputs

Canada is bounded by three oceans, the Atlantic on the east, the Arctic on the north, and the Pacific on the west. The Canadian shoreline is the longest in the world with a mainland coastline of 28,760 kilometers and an additional 67,327 kilometers of island coastline. With almost 10 million square kilometers of land

9

and freshwater area, it is second in size to the USSR and is 5 percent larger than the United States. The common border between the United States and Canada is 8,900 kilometers with 2,480 of these along the Alaskan boundary.

In spite of the many advantages of geographic location, Canada does suffer a handicap in that 90 percent of the country is north of the 50th parallel. This results in long, cold winters with limited hours of daylight. As a result of the cold climate, much of the northern land surface is permafrost, a combination of ice and frozen soil, which is unusable for agriculture and makes construction difficult.

The Canadian shield, the primary geological feature of the country, surrounds Hudson Bay and covers over half the country. The shield contains virtually every mineral on earth except those laid down under tropical conditions and is being increasingly tapped for its minerals, forests, and hydropower.[1] Hudson Bay is a large, shallow-water body in the northeast. Although not particularly important as far as resources go, Hudson Bay has been prominent in Canadian policy, and Canada has long claimed it as historic waters.

Canada's resource base is huge; in 1972 Canada was the world's largest producer of asbestos, silver, nickel, and zinc; was second in aluminum, cadmium, cobalt, magnesium, and wood pulp; and was third in gold, uranium, and lumber. The major marine resources are fisheries and offshore petroleum. The fish catch in 1972 was valued at $216,555,000, which was only 2 percent of the gross national product. However, the fishing industry employs over 100,000 people either directly in fishing or indirectly in activities such as processing and fishing-vessel support. This results in a strong interest group supporting certain policies. Canada is primarily a coastal fishery state, but sedentary and anadromous fisheries are also important. Canadian fishermen, under reciprocal Canadian-United States agreements, operate in United States waters in several areas, but Canada does not have a distant water fishery.

The Canadian continental shelf has vast oil and gas reserves. Much of this potential is in the Arctic Ocean, making exploitation hazardous and expensive. The remainder is primarily in the subarctic and temperate areas of the east coast. The continental shelf on the west coast is comparatively narrow with limited petroleum exploitation prospects.

The United States has been and will continue to be Canada's dominant trading partner. Most of the remainder of Canada's foreign trade is with Europe, but recently the emphasis has been shifting to Asian markets. All European and Asian trade and most United States trade is dependent on marine transportation. Foreign seaborne commerce amounted to 166 million metric tons in 1971. Exploitation of the Arctic region will place further emphasis on marine transportation since most of the resources in the Arctic will require vessel movement. Some oil and gas can be transported from the Arctic region by pipeline, but pipelines will only be competitive in the MacKenzie River area.

Processing

Canada possesses a relatively strong federal government, but the federal government is highly responsive to the concerns of the provinces, due in part to the residual sovereignty, which rests with the provinces. Many, including the current prime minister, refer to the present form of government as "cooperative federalism," a very apt description.

During the course of Canadian history, the populace has displayed a strong feeling of independence. This same feeling pervades much of the public philosophy regarding Canada's relationship with the United States. Although there is a strong feeling of friendship towards the United States and a desire to maintain close ties, there is also strong pressure to assert independence from the United States and ensure that the world is aware of this independence. Some Canadians see the United States as a threat to Canadian sovereignty and maintain that Canada cannot give the appearance of a satellite of the United States.[2] This feeling has resulted in strong pressure on the government to establish policy independent from that of the United States.

Environmental concerns are a strong element in Canadian policy. Canada is among the world's most environmentally conscious countries. Canada's relatively sparse population and the highly fragile nature of the Canadian arctic environment contribute to this consciousness. The permafrost can be damaged by man's activities; the damage may be irreversible. In some areas the permafrost shows damage several months after merely being walked on. Due to the high interdependence of the systems in the far north, ecological relationships can be easily disturbed and may take years to recover or may never recover from damages induced by man. The Arctic Ocean and shorelines also exhibit this fragile ecological balance.

Recently, there has been an attempt to involve nongovernment actors in the decision process. In 1972 the Institute for Research on Public Policy was established in Montreal as a private, nonprofit corporation to advise the federal government on policy matters. Some have compared the Institute to the Brookings Institution and the Rand Corporation in the United States.[3] However, the Institute is designed to cover a broader spectrum of policy than either Brookings Institution or the Rand Corporation. The Institute, which is not appended to any government unit, is designed to provide a nongovernment viewpoint on public policy.

The executive branch of the Canadian national government consists of the Cabinet headed by the prime minister. The size of the Cabinet varies, but is usually about 20 members. The federal Cabinet occupies the most powerful position in Canada for policy making; many analysts consider it the principal policy-making structure of the Canadian political system.[4] The executive authority is divided among the Cabinet ministers who head the agencies and departments of the executive branch. Most of the major policy decisions are made by the "inner cabinet" consisting of the prime minister, the minister of finance, and the head of the Treasury Board. When compared to the rest of the Cabinet, the minister of finance typically exerts a strong conservative influence on policy deliberations. The ministers of justice and the minister of external affairs also are important in the policy process, particularly for matters pertaining to their departments. Since marine policy invariably involves international considerations, the minister of external affairs is usually influential in marine policy decisions. In addition to the established departments and agencies that perform the executive functions, committees are used particularly for planning purposes and interdepartmental coordination.

There is no single agency or department that is responsible for marine affairs nor does one appear dominant; therefore, marine-policy formulation is accomplished by committees. The Interdepartmental Committee on Territorial Waters, established in 1932, is the expert body that handles issues related to maritime matters.[5] In 1970 the committee was reorganized as the Interdepartmental Committee on the Law of the Sea.[6] The composition of the committee is not fixed, but varies with reorganizations of the government and also with the particular issue under consideration. Typically, it might consist of members from the Department of External Affairs; National Defense; Energy, Mines and Resources; Environment; Industry, Trade and Commerce; Justice; Indian Affairs and Northern Development; Transportation; and the Ministry of State for Science and Technology. The Cabinet Committee on Priorities and Planning reviews and advises on major policy proposals.

Since the executive branch of government is an arm of the legislative branch, close coordination is possible within the federal government. It is normally possible to gain legislative support for action once the executive branch has made a decision on policy, particularly if the prime minister's party has a clear majority.

The government sometimes uses royal commissions to assist in policy making. The commissions are composed of respected, influential citizens and many times may be members of the Senate. In the past, royal commissions have been used both to gain support for a policy already decided upon and to assist in the decision process. The government also uses white-paper reports on major issues to speed the process by facilitating the information exchange between the government and the public.

Canada uses the planning, programming, and budget system (PPBS), similar to the system employed in the United States. Under PPBS, planning is done over an interval of time, normally five years. It is during this stage that initial policy formulation occurs. Policies are examined to determine whether existing and proposed programs are consistent with established policies. If not, either the program is changed or a proposal is generated to modify the policy. This is frequently the initiative for a policy decision; however, the decision could also be triggered by political concerns, leadership changes, philosophy of the leader, or other factors originating among the political leadership. The inputs, filters, and institutional arrangements that affect the decision have a high degree of continuity, that is, they usually continue for relatively long periods without major changes. The key actor in the major policy-decision process changes periodically. Although each will be affected by the same inputs, filters, and processes, individual differences can produce changes in policy.

Prime Minister Pierre Trudeau has been responsible for several major policy changes that affect marine policy. Analysis of his views permits better understanding of these decisions. Trudeau is a believer in systems analysis as an aid in decision making. He places heavy emphasis on planning and established a formalized planning unit in the prime minister's office. He also felt there was considerable room for improvement in government administration and streamlined procedures by reducing the Cabinet committees from 27 to 9, while vesting the committees with the responsibility and authority to make many of the final policy decisions previously made by the whole Cabinet. As part of his efforts to improve the government, he has sought greater public involvement in the determination of public policy. He referred to this as "participative democracy" and implemented it through a public awareness and education program. Trudeau also felt strongly that one of the goals of government should be to maximize the environmental quality. Trudeau has attempted to maintain an open atmosphere within the Cabinet and encouraged expression of opposing viewpoints through a multiple-advocacy approach.

Previous Canadian leaders have often been content to parallel United States policy. Trudeau strives for a unique Canadian policy. Trudeau also feels that, in spite of a relatively small population, Canada has a major role to play in international leadership. Because of conflicts with Canada's basic national interests, this end is not always possible, but it is pursued to the maximum extent possible.

Outputs

The end result of a decision process is a policy output. This may be development of a new policy, modification of an existing policy, or a decision not to make any change. Regardless of the nature of the decision, the outputs in marine policy may take a variety of forms, including assertion of domestic jurisdiction, control over marine activity, ratification or rejection of a treaty, support of a particular industry, maintenance of a naval force level, or rejection or acceptance of actions by other countries.

Traditionally, Canada followed the policy of the United States and Great Britain on territorial seas with the claim limited to three miles. In 1970 Canada amended the Territorial Sea and Fishing Zones Act and extended the territorial sea to 12 miles. This was a departure from prior Canadian policy which had emphasized multilateral rather than unilateral actions. However, it was rightly noted by Canada that the 12-mile claim was not a precedent, since a majority of countries had already claimed 12 or more miles.

In 1958, at the first United Nations Law of the Sea Conference, Canada attempted to get agreement on a three-plus-nine arrangement, that is, a three-mile territorial sea and a nine-mile contiguous zone.[7] When this failed, Canada campaigned for a six-plus-six formula a six-mile territorial sea and a six-mile contiguous zone.[8] Canada warned that the law was developing toward wider assertions of sovereignty and that some extension of jurisdiction beyond territorial seas was necessary. Canada had only belated and limited success in enlisting United States support for the proposal.

In 1960, at the second United Nations Law of the Sea Conference, Canada campaigned actively for the six-plus-six formula and, this time, was successful in obtaining United States' support. In spite of an active effort to broaden the base of support, the six-plus-six formula failed.[9] However, Canada, rather than abandoning the attempt, joined with Britain in canvassing numerous countries, asking them to join in a multilateral agreement based on the six-plus-six formula. Although they sought United States' assistance, the effort was unsuccessful. The canvass revealed that 40 countries would support such a proposal provided the United States and other major powers also agreed. The United States, when approached on this matter, did not consider the proposal timely or appropriate. Later, when the Canadian House of Commons was discussing the 12-mile territorial sea, Mitchell Sharp, minister of external affairs, stated that the limit was a sign of Canadianism, not anti-Americanism.

Another decision regarding unilateral action involves the Arctic archipelago. In this instance the output is not clearly defined and, in fact, may be classified as a no output decision. However, it is included here since it illustrates the marine policy-decision process pertaining to an established position and will probably be a cause of future statutory action.

Canadian claims to the islands in the archipelago are well established. In 1907 Senator Ponarier called for a formal declaration of possession by Canada of the lands and islands lying between the Dominion and the North Pole. In 1909 the government did assert that, if the islands were to be claimed by anyone, Canada would consider them all to be her own. In 1920 Canada claimed everything known and unknown between 60 and 141 degrees west longitude. By 1922 a station had been established on Ellesmere Island, and patrols were conducted to the other islands in the archipelago.

In 1958 the minister of northern affairs stated that the area to the north of Canada, including the islands and the waters between the islands and areas beyond, were Canadian. On 15 May 1969 Prime Minister Trudeau stated:

It is also known that not all countries would accept the view that the waters between the islands of the archipelago are internal waters over which Canada has full sovereignty. . . . Such differences, of course, would have to be settled not on an arbitrary basis but with due regard for established principles of international law.[10]

This position was severely criticized by several members of the House of Commons who felt Canada should assert an unequivocal claim to the archipelagic waters. A less equivocal view was expressed by Secretary of State Sharp during an interview outside the House of Commons on February 19, 1970. This position was reaffirmed in a Canadian note handed to the United States government on April 16, 1970, which indicated: "With respect to the waters of the Arctic Archipelago, the position of Canada has always been that these waters are regarded as Canadian."[11] Perhaps Canada would take stronger action to assert her archipelagic claim if her claim were seriously challenged, but so far this has not been the case.

On June 26, 1970 the Arctic Waters Pollution Prevention Act received unanimous consent in the House of Commons. The unanimous vote reveals the depth of feeling involved in the decision.[12] The act places controls on oil exploration and exploitation activities on the Arctic continental shelf and over vessels carrying oil within 100 miles of the Arctic coast. The vessel controls include not only design and construction requirements to prevent pollution but also movement controls within the zone. These vessel controls distinguish the act as a major unilateral action departing from the accepted international regime. It could also serve as a milestone for future controls, either unilateral or multilateral.

Canada originally attempted to obtain multilateral action through the Intergovernmental Maritime Consultative Organization (IMCO).[13] In November 1969 IMCO sponsored an international legal conference in Brussels on marine-pollution damage. Canada felt that the conference achieved only minimal results.[14] Secretary of State Sharp expressed Canada's reaction to the Brussels Conference when he summarized the events leading up to the Arctic Waters Pollution Prevention Act:

Many delegations at Brussels displayed what appeared to us to be an excessive caution and conservatism and a rigid pre-occupation with the traditional concept of unqualified freedom of the high seas. That freedom, in our eyes, seemed to be tantamount to a licensee [sic] to pollute; it did not in any way strike a proper balance between the interest of the flag state in unfettered rights of navigation and the fundamental interest of the coastal state in the integrity of its shores.[15]

Canada's attempts at Brussels to incorporate preventive measures in the conventions failed, resulting in the adoption only of remedial measures.

In October 1969 it was becoming evident to Canada that her position would not be accepted during the Brussels conference. Just before the conference convened, the governor-general, in a Speech from the Throne on October 23, 1969, discussed the precarious nature of the polar regions and referred to Canada's responsibility to preserve the undespoiled polar areas. The following day Prime Minister Trudeau asserted that Canada would protect the Arctic environment from pollution. It was clear that Canada was prepared to act unilaterally if the Brussels conference failed to produce acceptable results.

During the House of Commons debates on enactment of the Arctic Waters Pollution Prevention Act, Secretary Sharp indicated the proposed action would not rule out the possibility of developing international arrangements for the preservation of the Arctic regions. He described the bill as a stepping stone toward the elaboration on an international legal order for the protection and preservation of the planet earth. During the debate it was also made clear that the controls were not designed to eliminate exploitation and use of the Arctic but to ensure that usage would not harm the environment.

Analysis and Conclusions

The Canadian policy process and the application of the model are well illustrated by the Arctic Waters Pollution Prevention Act. The inputs that were important in this situation were shoreline length, area of the continental shelf, and fishery resources within the 200-mile zone. All of these inputs favored the action. Seaborne trade might have been a counter force; however, it was made clear that the action would not prohibit vessel activity but would require strong controls on vessel activity. In the case of the action on archipelagic waters the same factors were important.

Several important filters strongly influenced the action. One of the strongest of these was foreign ownership of Canadian industry. Without this filter industry's heavy dependence on seaborne trade would make Canada a strong advocate of freedom of the seas. This input was also influenced by the carriage of the trade. Excluding the Great Lakes trade, Canada moves less than 1 percent of her foreign trade in Canadian vessels. It is clear that Canada views herself as a coastal state, not a shipping state. Tighter vessel controls will have an adverse impact on seaborne trade, but it appears the other inputs and strong filters modify the seaborne trade input.

Several other filters played major roles in the decisions. Two of these were the environmental concern and the strong public desire to assert independence from Washington. These were consistent with Trudeau's philosophy and public pressure bearing on the government. A closely related filter was the desire of Canada to assume a world leadership position in matters relating to environmental protection and law of the sea. The voyage of the SS *Manhattan* was an extremely important factor since it focused public attention on the problem. This public awareness may not have changed the outcome, but it did produce a feeling of urgency that caused prompt action. In the case of the territorial-sea claim, the fishery interests and concentration of voting strength in the coastal regions were very important.

The Case of the People's Republic of China

Background

The People's Republic of China (PRC) is not noted principally as a naval or maritime power. Compared to the United States or the Soviet Union, this is probably a correct assessment. In spite of this relative lack of seapower, it would be foolish to ignore the marine posture of China. In the future, the PRC, like the United States and the USSR, will have to be included in any serious discussion of questions concerning international marine affairs. Prediction of China's elevation to superpower status in a multipolar world has become far more believable in the last decade.

Inputs

Historically, national interest in the sea has been measured by the size of the navy, merchant-shipping tonnage, and fish catch. Once this was an adequate formulation, but the complex marine environment of today requires the analysis of different types of marine attributes.

Based on geographic factors alone, China has ample reason to pursue marine interests vigorously. The PRC's land area is 9,596,961 square kilometers, among the top five in the world. Of this, 6,400 kilometers, or 21 percent of the national boundary, is oceanic coastline bordering on three seas. The 200-meter isobath encompasses 60,865 square kilometers of continental shelf, and a 200-nautical-mile boundary on the shelf includes 727,790 square kilometers. The fisheries within these limits are estimated at a maximum sustainable yield (MSY) of between 5 and 12 million metric tons, certainly among the richest in the world.

Fisheries are not China's only marine wealth. Among other resources are petroleum reserves estimated at 1.5 million metric tons on the shelf.[16] Other shelf resources are believed to be extensive. To a lesser extent, China has also used the sea for trade amounting to an estimated $6 to $8 billion in 1974, and a registered merchant-ship tonnage approaching 2,600,000 deadweight, or 1,871,000 gross registered tons.[17] To these figures must be added domestic waterborne trade, roughly estimated at 160–170,000,000 metric tons for 1974.[18]

Processing

In analyzing government policies affecting the marine environment, one must concentrate on the external manifestations of that policy. It would be interesting to explore Peking's internal decision making and develop a paradigm to explain the process, but there is a paucity of relevant information. However, an attempt can be made to explore selected policy decisions, relate them to basic inputs and filters, and test them for consistency against the apparent goals of the Chinese regime.

To place the inputs into the proper context, it is necessary to consider the background situation and inputs or filters that may affect interpretation. Three types of filters are considered. First are the historical filters that influence Chinese perceptions and affect a key element in decision making—the value system of the leaders and the nation. Second are the physical and economic data that overlap and amplify the inputs. Third are present government ideology, organization, methodology, and principal goals, that is, the actual processing mechanism for the inputs. No discussion of policy can afford to neglect the biases imposed on the Chinese by time and environment. A very old civilization, China has developed a complex set of intuitive and perceptual filters, which form the basis for a distinctively different value system affecting policies in all areas.

China entered the eighteenth century aloof from the world, protected by natural barriers, and possessing a highly developed culture with a pronounced economic, political, military, and naval superiority, which recognized no equal, needed no allies, and permitted no outside competition. The feelings of superiority nurtured by this dominance seem to have become an ingrained part of the Chinese heritage. Only incursions from the sea by Western powers in the eighteenth and ninteenth centuries forced the recognition of more powerful nations.[19] This Western incursion emphasized technology rather than the highly developed moral philosophy so prized by the Chinese.[20]

Aside from general filters, China's attitude toward the sea appears to have been dominated by two major economic and military influences. Economically, China has obtained great wealth from the sea. Fish are plentiful along much of the extensive Chinese coastline. Fishing is an ancient occupation and has been an integral part of the economy for centuries. Additionally, in recent years the continental shelf has promised great wealth. However, the sea has also posed a threat. Invaders of China for the past three centuries have encroached from the sea; no Chinese navy has been able to stop them.[21] This experience has been reinforced by the confrontation with the United States over Taiwan in 1958 and the presence of Soviet fleets in more recent crises.[22] In spite of this harassment, marine policies that further the goals perceived by national leadership have been adopted.

The principal orientation of PRC is still toward the land. This is clearly illustrated by the composition of the PRC's armed forces, the People's Liberation Army (PLA). Of the four arms of the PLA, the land-warfare component is the largest, most important politically, and most powerful militarily. The naval component is the smallest and weakest, surpassed in size by the army, strategic missile force, and air force. Since the PLA is a political force in the PRC, this distribution of power appears to be significant.[23]

China is accessible from the sea through at least 8 ports and 11 major rivers. The rivers, especially the Yellow, Yangtze, and Pearl, provide access to the interior of China and are indispensable to the transportation system. The ports provide the Chinese mainland terminus for most foreign trade, with Shanghai possibly the most important port. The proximity of other land masses to China's coastline was once of little consequence. Today Japan, in addition to being one of Peking's chief competitors for Asian leadership, is also a main trading partner. Korea and Vietnam have been testing grounds for Chinese power. Taiwan, not considered herein and ostensibly a Chinese province, South Vietnam, and South Korea are allies of one of China's chief antagonists. Even the Philippines, Indonesia, Malaysia, and smaller countries now compete for fisheries, rights on the continental shelf, and territories that the PRC claims. All of these countries influence PRC marine policy.

Few countries have a large segment of the population living near the coast without also having an allied interest in the sea. Over 80 percent of the population of mainland China, about 716 million people, lives in the eastern third of the country. Population density on rural coastlines is almost without exception over 100 persons per square kilometer and frequently closer to 500. In cities it ranges to over 1 million per square kilometer.[24] From Shanghai south, the people are far more conscious of the ocean, have historically used the water to a greater extent, and tend to be more dependent on the sea than the northerners. Since the ruling power in the CCP (Chinese Communist Party) has had a heavy northern and inland bias, the ocean orientation of the southern provinces has less influence at the national level than otherwise might be the case.[25]

Within a complex party and state bureaucracy with its new communist and old national heritage, the decisions regarding marine policy are made. Upon establishment of the People's Republic of China in 1949, the primary goals of the CCP and the new government were already well developed. The goals apparently included and still include:

1. Completion, or in Mao Tse-Tung's word, "continuation," of the revolution.
2. Reestablishment of control over all territories and areas considered to be Chinese
3. Limitation of or end to Western influence in China and the Far East[26]

The political ideology and organization of a national government usually has a major influence on short- and long-term marine policy. This is true for the People's Republic of China. The present Communist government, as in the case of the dynastic governments, is highly authoritarian, hierarchal, and centralized.[27] Even while professing a Communist ideology, it may be as much a traditional Chinese government as a Communist government because of the strong resemblance to the historic Chinese model.[28]

Although the principal goals already enumerated shape the pattern into which all actions and policies must be integrated, certain issues have forced themselves on the Chinese leadership as matters of urgency. National security has required the continued attention of the leadership. Most of the top leaders participated extensively in the war against the Nationalists; their military backgrounds would not let them ignore real or imagined threats from the United States or the Soviet Union. Possibly the most complex issue is the constant emphasis that must be placed on food production just to offset population increases. Out of necessity and to establish credibility, the PRC has had to place agricultural production at the top of priority lists or see its programs fail. Placing agriculture first has obviously slowed both light and heavy industrial expansion.[29]

One functional area in which decisions have been made regarding marine policy is exploitation of the living and nonliving resources of the sea. Interest in fishing and natural resources on the continental shelf has forced decisions concerning exploitation of ocean resources and definition of the areas to be exploited. The apparent policies include:

1. Exploit fisheries to the maximum sustainable yield in waters immediately adjacent to mainland China
2. Employ little or no long-distance fishing
3. Protect the resources of seabed areas immediately adjacent to the coast for PRC use and limit immediate exploitation.[30]

The decisions about fishing appear to indicate general and specific policy made at high levels and intended for long-term application. Neither was a departure in policy from the previous regime, but they were later supplemented by a decision to give priority to production of food. This was apparently translated by the Ministry of Agriculture and Forestry into higher fish quotas. Since any Chinese decision concerning food is of a priority nature, there is always urgency involved, but barring large-scale foreign invasion of fisheries, urgency concentrates on size of the quotas rather than other decisions.[31]

In setting production quotas there appears to be flexibility with information exchanged between ministry and local officials. Nevertheless, the fishermen are apparently hard pressed to meet the quotas the ministry sets.[32]

For nonliving ocean resources, there is equally good evidence that active decisions have been made. Along with the stand on fisheries, published statements have outlined China's position on the continental-shelf issue supporting exclusive economic zones of at least 200 or more miles and fisheries zones extending to 200 nautical miles.[33] It appears that the highest level membership of the party and the government made the decision, since strongly worded official policy statements were issued publicly when United States-Japanese plans for exploitation were revealed in 1970.[34] Initially, there was no great urgency about seabed exploitation in Asia generally, although Peking has been aware of oil deposits for at least ten years. The surveys completed about 1970 by various United States oil companies changed the situation. When action became necessary to protect important resources, policy and claims were immediately made public.[35]

The decisions regarding China's interest in shelf resources must be considered rational by almost any standards. The purpose of the decisions and actions was clear from the beginning, that is, to retain control of shelf resources by nullifying outside claims, particularly those of Japan. It was the pressures from other states making unilateral claims that forced Peking to set forth its policy.[36] There is little evidence to indicate that the PRC will become a major exploiter of the nonliving continental-shelf resources in the near future, although some attempts are already underway. The technology to drill for oil under water is in use, but land sources have not been fully exploited. The technology for deep-sea mining is still being developed, so it is also unlikely that the PRC will be actively mining on a large scale. But the policy does provide protection for the future.

In the analysis of sea resources, quantitative inputs logically explain PRC policy. The long coastline, area, proximity, and richness of the continental shelf make it a highly desirable, exclusive possession. The press of population increase, the energy and other resources required to support a population approaching 1 billion people, the desire to gradually improve the living conditions of the peasant and to modernize industry, strongly favor adoption of a policy that protects ocean wealth from outside exploitation. For example, if fishing supplies only 4 percent of protein requirements, as indicated by United Nations estimates, at least 36 million Chinese depend on fish for protein.[37] Even if the percentage of fish protein does not increase, total requirements will as population increases by 16–18 million people annually. Bad years in agriculture could increase pressure on fishing.

Based on past production, the Food and Agricultural Organization of the United Nations and Nationalist Chinese estimates, mainland China had a 1974 catch of about 7.0 million metric tons. Of this, 4.6 million metric tons was estimated to have come from internal waters and 2.6 million metric tons from coastal waters. Some earlier estimates would reverse the percentage catch from the two sources.[38] Assuming a roughly equivalent value to the United States saltwater catch, which was at least 100,000 tons less, saltwater catch could have been worth as much as $1 billion, or nearly 1 percent of GNP, and total catch should approach $2.2 billion, or 1.5 percent of GNP. In spite of food requirements and catch value, economics would not seem to support investment for distant water fishing.

The importance of shelf resources of oil and minerals can likewise be supported by the inputs. To supplement domestic food stocks and obtain technology, Peking has been importing grain and sophisticated goods, but balance of payments has become a problem. Oil production and petrochemicals could reduce the balance of payments deficit and enable China to obtain the required food and technology. The PRC became an oil exporter in 1972 when land production reached about 30 million metric tons. Shelf production will doubtless be used for the same purpose in the future.[39] Oil is obviously important, too, in helping the PRC modernize its own economy and raise the Chinese standard of living. GNP and industrialization could be radically advanced in the years to come by bringing shelf deposits of oil into production.

A second major historical indicator of national ocean interests is the maritime industry including shipping, ship-building, and port development. Active decisions regarding these industries have been made by the government as a matter of necessity. They have had the effect of:

1. Gradually increasing the size of the merchant marine with Chinese-built ships and chartered vessels
2. Improving port facilities for commercial-shipping operations
3. Building the internal sea-transport system of mainland China
4. Increasing the value, but limiting international trade to the value of exports[40]

Each of these mutually supportive decisions seems to have been an active, high-level, long-term decision aimed at strengthening China's foreign policy options and promoting a closely controlled foreign trade. They indicate recognition of the desirability of increasing foreign trade, although motivation is still primarily to import necessary technology or food, and assist foreign policy rather than to engage in large-scale trading.[41]

Peking's decision to develop a more modern and capable merchant marine to handle increasing world trade appears to be very rational. The goal of Third World leadership is aided by introducing the Chinese presence into other countries in a nonthreatening manner while the export of goods to balance the import of food and technology is mandatory.[42] Use of trade and shipping remains centered around these two purposes, but also helps to modernize an industrial activity in which the PRC has previously been lagging. Thus, these decisions that place more emphasis on shipping and trade are logical and favorable to foreign policy plans, economic health, and industrial expansion. It is difficult to believe under these circumstances that China would neglect her maritime industry altogether.

Any development that helps to employ the population in labor-intensive industries and increases the size of the GNP is desirable; shipping and trade are capable of helping the economy on both counts. Income from foreign trade is presently estimated at 4 percent of GNP or about $6 billion in 1974, with some estimates as high as $8 billion or 5 percent.[43] This is an increase of more than two and a half times since 1950. Estimating seaborne transportation at about 1.5 percent of GNP, or $2.1 billion, the total income is a worthwhile addition to China's income. The growth rate for foreign trade is predicted to be about 5 percent, or 1 percent greater than the economy as a whole, and the increase in registered shipping tonnage recently has averaged above 10 percent annually.[44] Construction and acquisition of commercial vessels has increased over 26 percent in the past four years. Estimates indicate that gross registered tonnage has more than doubled since 1968 to more than 1.8 million tons in 1974.[45] There was a lag of nearly seven years between completion of the first three 10,000-ton, mainland China-built ships. In 1969 four ships were launched and at least five more in 1970.[46] Construction has evidently continued although the actual number of ships being built is unknown.

Outputs

Policy making in regard to territorial claims appears to be quite consistent, whether the territory in question is landlocked, as was the case in the Sino-Indian and Sino-Soviet disputes, or surrounded by water, as in the more recent controversy over the Paracel and Spratley Islands. A series of active decisions at high party levels characterizes territorial claims. In 1954 the PRC published a map stating specific long-term claims to large land and sea areas, including Taiwan, the Po Hai Gulf, and several groups of islands that figure prominently in marine policy. There was probably no internal dissent about the claims since they are long-standing and consistent with the pre-1949 claims of the Nationalist government.[47] However, within the government there has probably been some discussion about possible major power reprisals resulting from the claims.

Current issues, including the 200-mile economic zone and the width of territorial seas, have given a value to many small island groups disproportionate to their economic worth. Islands that were formerly rather primitive bases for fishing vessels now have the promise of wealth from oil on their shelves and exclusive fishing in their waters. In the case of the Paracels, Spratleys, Senkakus, and Macclesfield Bank, strategic position on major trade routes adds to the value. The island claims are of long standing so it is doubtful if current marine considerations alone have forced adoption of the present policy, which did not really change as a result of the Communist takeover except to become firmer.[48]

Another important indicator of national marine interest is naval power. In this area three basic decisions seem to have been made about the PRC's requirements for naval forces:

1. Naval forces are necessary to protect the mainland, adjacent waters, and island possessions from oceanic threats.
2. Naval forces should be defensive in nature with limited capability to project power beyond the immediate defensive zone.
3. Numerical advantage should be used to compensate for limited technical advancement and size of units.

These are long-term, high-level decisions applying to all naval forces. Limits on the mission, size, and expenditures for a navy were probably concurred in by most leaders because there were insufficient resources to do otherwise. Since the naval arm of the PLA already existed, any urgent expansion was designed to strengthen the navy against the United States-Nationalist threat. Present or future intent to radically change the structure, missions, or composition is not apparent, although evidence of growth in the shipbuilding program does exist.[49]

The specific objectives of a decision to build a defensive navy was obviously to provide the naval capability necessary (within resource limitations) to protect PRC interests at sea, provide defense at sea against perceived foreign threats to the mainland, and project the image of a powerful China. The protracted war with the Nationalists made Communist leadership aware of the military necessity and political advantages of having credible naval forces to counter national security threats. Initially, the most serious threat perceived by the PRC was the United States, whose backing of the Nationalists was probably a very real reminder of previous foreign incursions from the sea.[50] Combined with the Nationalist threat and the recollection of earlier defeats, the United States presence probably reinforced the decision to limit the navy to defensive and amphibious capabilities. It has not, however, prevented the building of a naval force larger than the British navy, including 7 destroyers, 13 frigates, 49 submarines, and 670 patrol boats, of which at least 106 mount cruise missile armament.[51]

Analysis of the inputs reinforces the propriety of the basic decisions. Expenditures of resources for naval force to protect 6,400 kilometers of sea boundaries and numerous islands are certainly warranted. Living resources of the water over China's shelf are extensive and attract distant fishing fleets. Surveys of the seabed on the shelf indicate desirable natural resources. A growing population of 895 million people is a strong argument for protecting these resources. Credible naval forces are a major way to show intense interest and prevent foreign exploitation of adjacent sea areas.

Future leadership may perceive the need for naval development as occurred with the Soviet Union. The PRC already possesses the third largest submarine force in the world, but if such a decision for expansion is made, significant long range capability with other than submarines will probably be a decade away. The building program appears to include 3 destroyers, 20 patrol craft, 4 conventional submarines, and 1 nuclear submarine, but no known large logistic support vessels. Even with the building program, it is doubtful if the navy's budget exceeds 25-30 percent of an estimated $14.5 billion defense budget, or about $4-$5 billion.[52]

Marine policy in the PRC must meet the test of being good national policy as well as good marine policy. Integrating marine policy into national policy can have a very beneficial effect in obtaining a consistent and compatible overall policy on land and sea. However, it is possible that marine issues could become stepchildren of the government if the leaders do not understand the importance of the sea. Peking has played the role of defender of the underdeveloped nations in the law of the sea discussions. In the ongoing struggle for marine resources and a new law of the sea, China will likely continue to take the position that the Soviet Union and the United States are imperialistic superpowers trying to dominate and exploit the sea for their own benefit. On the other hand, Peking will emphasize its own empathy with underdeveloped countries by defending the Third World position.[53]

China did not participate in the creation of the present law of the sea, has ratified none of the 1958 Geneva Conventions and does not consider them binding. In fact, China does not consider itself bound by any laws not specifically ratified or recognized. Consequently, faced frequently with conflicts between its desires and international law, Peking has endorsed the principle of absolute state sovereignty, a concept that allows a state to disregard the parts of international law with which it does not agree.[54] Although China may be out of the mainstream of modern aspects of international law, the People's Republic does recognize five principles of peaceful coexistence as the basis of a modern law of nations.

1. Mutual respect for territorial integrity and sovereignty
2. Nonaggression
3. Mutual noninterference in each other's internal affairs
4. Equality and mutual benefit
5. Peaceful coexistence

These principles are apparently considered applicable to all interstate relations and probably form the basis for China's approach to the law of the sea as well.[55] Since 1958 the PRC has claimed a 12-nautical-mile territorial sea. In amplifying that policy, China has argued that every nation has the right to determine the breadth of its territorial sea almost without limit. A strait, even if an international waterway, should come under the jurisdiction of the state in whose territorial sea it is located. Although merchant vessels have a right to transit straits if they comply with coastal state regulations, warships are required to give extended advance notice and have prior permission before any strait transit through territorial seas regardless of purpose.[56] Likewise, Peking maintains that coastal states have the right to define exclusive fisheries zones adjacent to territorial waters out to a maximum distance of 200 nautical miles. An international organization would have jurisdiction beyond that, but not impinge on national sovereignty. This position on fisheries zones is strongly influenced by two factors already mentioned, the wealth of fishing grounds adjacent to China's coast, and the desire to keep foreigners away from the rich coastal waters.[57]

Conclusions

Based solely on the magnitude of the inputs, the People's Republic of China would be expected to have a strong interest in the sea. Predictably, from inputs and due to processing filters, the level of interest is uneven. PRC claims for territorial waters, exclusive economic zone, fisheries zone, and its stance on other law of the sea issues are outputs consistent with those expected of a developing state.

The PRC has not ratified the 1958 Geneva Law of the Sea, 1954 IMCO Pollution Conventions, or any of the international conventions on marine-related issues, except for those of a purely technical nature, such as the 1948 Convention for the Prevention of Accidents at Sea and the 1930 International Load Line Convention. Animosity between China and the maritime powers, particularly the United States, has caused Peking to take the position that many of these agreements were contrary to Chinese interests.[58]

The naval arm of the PRC is composed of 51 submarines, 14 ships of frigate size or larger displacing about 188,000 tons, and more than 1,200 smaller ships including 680 fast combatants mounting guns or missiles and displacing 190,000 tons. It also includes 450 aircraft. The mission is principally defensive, only submarines are capable of operating far from the Chinese coast.[59] Naval size is a logical outgrowth from inputs that include a long, resource-rich coastline and a large shelf area to police and patrol.

In the next few years, Communist China will be undergoing major changes in leadership precipitated by the deaths of Chou En-lai and Mao Tse-tung. There is no guarantee that the transition will be smooth. Since 1949, in spite of leadership purges, the PRC has maintained a consistent, long-range marine policy. A policy consensus must have existed among top level leaders, even though there have been short-term inconsistencies in execution. It is questionable if the same cohesiveness will continue to exist in the future. Assuming that future leadership carries on similar policies, there will still be an evolutionary process at work. Natural calamities or an increased military burden would probably produce some redirection. However, based on the present input-output trends some predictions can be made.

First, China will continue a gradual increase in merchant-fleet size. National resources, size, population, accessibility to the sea, and national objectives indicate probable greater involvement in international affairs. Increases in fishing-fleet size and catch are likely to continue to be high on China's priority list, although distant water fishing is improbable. This may mean further treaty restrictions for other nations fishing Chinese waters, particularly if a 200-mile, exclusive economic zone becomes standard, or if fish stocks become inadequate. Disagreements will be solved to Peking's satisfaction through diplomatic action and covert pressure rather than overt military action. Adoption of a 200-mile economic-zone width might also foreshadow attempts to rewrite certain marine boundary claims. There is no sign that China is satisfied with present conditions in regard to shelf boundaries, and the possibility exists that this could become an area of additional dispute. Chinese marine territorial claims to Taiwan and other islands will continue to be a source of friction.

Marine expansion should increase the possibility of some softening or subtle changes in position on law of the sea issues, such as passage through straits. If changes in position are preempted by enactment of a new international law of the sea agreement, further bilateral or multilateral treaties would be in order.

In spite of the speculation about increased marine interest, immediate re-allocation of resources to marine programs and government investment is not likely to occur. Much of the budget is committed to ongoing programs that do not permit funding reductions. Manifestations of increased interest will probably be gradual.

Should the People's Republic of China continue present trends for an extended period, only one ingredient of seapower is missing, that is, a larger navy capable of protecting worldwide interests. This analysis would seem to have China approaching a crossroads similar to that faced by another land power, the Soviet Union, immediately following World War II. Increasing international trade, a growing merchant fleet, an important fishing industry, and ambitions to lead the Third World seem to point to further gradual expansion of a navy that is already the sixth or seventh largest in the world. In spite of Peking's protestations, it may be difficult to avoid competing militarily with the other major powers. In spite of considerable differences, the parallels between the current Chinese position and that of the Soviet Union following World War II, coupled with predictions of a multipolar world with several superpowers, are interesting to contemplate.[60]

The Case of Iran

Background

In several respects the situation in the Persian Gulf and the Indian Ocean region today is reminiscent of that before Western entry by the Portuguese. No great power touches its shore; its sea lanes exist because of markets beyond its limits. The trading pattern has remained overwhelmingly external rather than intra-regional. The navies of the riparian states are weak when judged against those of the great powers. The new political patterns that have emerged with the decline of empires since World War II have highlighted those conflicting territorial claims and other traditional rivalries that were submerged during the period of European hegemony.

In the Gulf, Iran sits atop an estimated 60 billion barrels of crude oil, or roughly one-tenth of the world's proven reserves.[61] The disposition of this product and the resulting revenues are in the firm hands of one man: His Imperial Majesty Mohammed Reza Pahlavi (the Shah of Iran). The Shah and his developing nation today play a key role in the power politics of the Middle East and the world. Iran is now producing 6.1 million barrels of oil daily and is second only to Saudi Arabia in oil exports. Its oil revenues are increasing astronomically. No other member of the group of suddenly wealthy oil nations is able to match Iran's projected scale of social and economic growth over the next two decades. The Shah's underlying aim in building his Great Civilization is to make Iran both secure and self-sufficient. His foreign policy is subsumed in an ever-widening world conception of relationships, a vision that includes an Iran at the apex of an Australasian-African triangle.

Theoretically, at least, Iran is a constitutional monarchy, with a parliament consisting of the Majlis or lower house, a senate, and premier. In fact, the Shah is one of the world's few remaining absolute monarchs. He guides all of Iran's essential business and is the ultimate authority on policy matters. But this simplification must not be allowed to conceal the fact that a government consists of a conglomerate of semifeudal, loosely allied organizations, each with a substantial life of its own.

In seven years of debate the United Nations General Assembly, the Ad Hoc and Permanent Seabed Committees and Sub-Committees, and the Third U.N. Law of the Sea Conference generated a considerable body of documents reflecting the public policy of over 100 states concerning the law of the sea. Iranian expressions of opinion, inclusive and exclusive claims, treaties and various other outputs, reflect specific Iranian positions and policies that defend and promote the marine interests of Iran.

Vital for any analysis of ocean affairs is an understanding of which aspects of international marine law and policy are of special concern to Iran. Problems of perception and of the decision-making process with respect to Iran's national marine policies are particularly pertinent and current, since efforts to conclude a viable law of the sea regime will be effective only to the extent that the regime can accommodate the real-world aspirations of states. Iran, in its dominant role in the Persian Gulf, provides a key "window" to a new and comprehensive legal order for the uses of the sea.

Marine Attributes of Iran

After centuries of living in the shadow of its illustrious Persian heritage, Iran has emerged once again as a power in the Middle East and as a voice in world affairs. Iran is now moving unevenly toward the ambitious goals set by Shah Mohammed Reza Pahlavi, Western-level prosperity at home and major-power status in the world. The Shah, who rules Iran with an authoritarian hand, says that within a generation there will be a "great civilization" in Iran equal economically and politically to most of the industrialized nations with an influence in the world that Iran has not had in two millennia, since the kingdoms of Darius and Cyrus reached Africa, Europe, and the Indian subcontinent.[62] Buttressed by oil and arms, Iran has become the self-appointed guardian of the Persian Gulf, a region whose oil resources exert a profound influence upon the world economy.

Iran, generally considered a Middle Eastern country, occupies some 636,000 square miles—about one-fifth the size of the United States—and is part of the enormous Middle East land mass of over 2.5 million square miles penetrated by the arms of the Mediterranean Sea, the Persian Gulf, and the Red Sea. Most of the country consists of the Iranian plateau, demarcated from the rest of the Middle East by the Zagros Mountains. The Persian Gulf is a shallow body of water covering the low lands between the Iranian plateau and the Arabian peninsula. It is an arm of the Indian Ocean that stretches to the heart of the Middle East, covering an area of some 97,000 square miles.[63] About half the size of the Caspian Sea and two-thirds the size of the Baltic Sea, the Gulf's total length is about 500 miles. Its width varies from about 180 miles at points between Iran and Abu Dhabi to about 21 miles at the Strait of Hormuz between Larak Island off the Iranian coast and the Great Quain Island off the Musandam peninsula in Oman. The Gulf is generally shallow with a maximum depth of about 300 feet. The entire seabed of the Persian Gulf, together with that of the adjoining Gulf of Oman, constitutes a single continental shelf whose edge or first fall-off appears not in the Gulf proper but in an area south of the Strait of Hormuz, where the submerged land beneath the Persian Gulf and the Gulf of Oman drops abruptly towards the Indian Ocean.

Iran has seven major and six minor ports. With the exception of Bandar 'Abbas, which is situated in the Strait of Hormuz, all of the remaining major ports are located near the head of the Persian Gulf. Abadan, Bandar-e Mah Shahr, and Kharg Island are petroleum ports, developed and maintained by the petroleum industry. In 1972 the country inaugurated a mammoth oil-loading terminal on the west coast of Kharg Island. Designed for the new generation of super tankers, the offshore twin-berth terminal is capable of doubling Iran's oil-exporting capacity.[64]

Iran is dependent upon sea transport both for the carriage of its crude oil exports and for the transport of virtually all consumer-product imports. The Iranian merchant fleet, however, carries only a small portion of this trade. The merchant fleet consists of approximately 23 ships (1,000 GRT or over) totaling about 310,000 DWT. The fleet, although small, is owned in part by the government.

Maritime laws and regulations are administered by the Ministry of Economy. To qualify for Iranian-flag registration, a ship must be owned either by an Iranian national or by an Iranian corporation with registered Iranian shareholders owning more than 50 percent of the capital shares. Iran is a member of the Inter-Governmental Maritime Consultative Organization (IMCO) and a party to the 1960 Safety of Life at Sea Convention. Iranian fleet development has been progressive. Iran currently has ship orders with Japan for supertankers and with Bulgaria, Rumania, and the United Kingdom for smaller frieghters.[65] In 1970 a maritime academy was established at Bushehr for the training of personnel for service in the merchant marine and in department of Ports and Navigation.

Iran's marine-fishing activities are confined to the Persian Gulf and the Sea of Oman. A notable proportion of the national catch, however, is taken in inland waters, especially from the Caspian Sea. The fisheries in the Gulf and the Sea of Oman are mainly characterized by rather primitive, small-scale operations. However, the Southern Fisheries Company, a semiautonomous government joint-stock company, is in the process of developing a significant national fishery in this area for shrimp, the most valuable resource of these waters. The previous practice of licensing foreign fishing operations is being discontinued transforming the fishery into a purely Iranian one. To this end, the Southern Fisheries Company has acquired a 3,700-ton factory ship and fifteen modern shrimp trawlers.[66] The Caspian Sea fisheries are managed by the Iranian National Fisheries Company, which is responsible to the Ministry of Agriculture and has acquired a 1,100-ton, modern mother ship and six catcher vessels to exploit resources of kilka for the production of fish meal or canned products.

Iran's fish catch, estimated at about 22,000 metric tons annually, is only a fraction of 1 percent of GNP and is insignificant in terms of food intake (per-capita consumption being probably less than 1 kg per annum).[67] Although some resources are already heavily exploited, the potential for the Persian Gulf fishing industry appears good. A survey by Japanese experts estimated that the industry could earn $200 million a year for Iran.[68]

Processing

Iran, a constitutional monarchy, has undergone rapid social change and a re-orientation in foreign policy in the past decade while maintaining a high degree of political stability. The constitution of Iran is composed of the Fundamental Law of 1906, the Supplementary Fundamental Law of 1907, and subsequent amendments. Since 1907 the constitution has been amended only four times; it has proved flexible and imprecise enough to retain its usefulness even as Iran has become a rapidly developing and modernizing state.

The executive arm of the government is headed by the Shah, who designates the prime minister and the cabinet members. He also convenes and dissolves Parliament, sets the course of policy in internal and external affairs, personally commands the armed forces, and has wide appointment powers. This bicameral legislature consists of an elected lower house, the Majlis; and a half-elected, half-royally appointed Senate. Members of the Parliament serve four-year terms. The parliamentary system of ministerial responsibility is provided for by the constitution and the prime minister with cabinet members subject to question by Parliament.[69]

The dominant position of the Iranian executive results from a strong authoritarian tradition along with intense loyalty to and awe of the monarchy. There is no tradition in Iran of having direct lines of responsibility from the prime minister to the ministries. The ministers are more likely to consider themselves answerable to the Shah than to the prime minister.[70] At the local level, Iran has had a strongly centralized system of government in which local and provincial officials remain largely dependent on Teheran for decision making and financial assistance. Efforts to improve and decentralize the government and to achieve greater public participation are progressing gradually.

Both politics and government have traditionally centered around personal contacts, influence, and the force of personality rather than institutions or political parties.[71] For a decade, however, the Shah has been building modern economic and social institutions by encouraging personnel selection based on ability. Thus traditional and modern forces can be seen at every level of political power in Iran—they are forced by the Shah to work together.

The importance of Iran in the world economy rests on its role as the fourth largest producer of crude petroleum, behind the United States, the USSR, and Saudi Arabia. Iran's political stability in the turbulent Middle East has been reflected by its willingness to fill gaps in the world oil supply created by war and by politically inspired cutbacks by other Middle East producers. Between 1961 and 1971, petroleum exports expanded at an average rate of 14.5 percent annually, as compared with 10.1 percent for the remainder of the Middle East.[72] Iran's importance as a world petroleum supplier is assured for the near future; its reserves are estimated at about 10 percent of the world total. Similarly, natural gas reserves are the third largest in the world and provide opportunities for greatly expanded output.

Iran's contemporary policy positions are no mere reflection of the conjunction of domestic and external political considerations. As a rapidly modernizing nation, Iran's "vital interests" in the Gulf extend beyond the safety of the existing regime vis-à-vis the perceived threat of Arab revolution and the historical desire to extend Iranian influence in the Gulf. Iran's contemporary interests in the Gulf are also rooted in economics.[73] Although the bulk of Iran's export trade consists of crude oil and petroleum products, trade in nonoil products also increases the Gulf's significance for Iran as the vital channel to world markets. For these reasons, Fifth Plan projects include studies covering modern agricultural development, exploitation of mines, irrigation, desalination of sea water, establishment of light and heavy industry, the development of communications, sea and food resources, and modern port facilities to solve the multifaceted needs of the Persian Gulf area.

Iran's heavy reliance on uninterrupted sea transport creates a degree of vulnerability. Since the British departure from the Gulf, this very dependence on the Persian Gulf for access to the Indian Ocean seemed to dictate that Iran would become its de facto guardian. In the past decade the evolution of Iranian military and economic power has changed Iran's regional policy from one of reaction to assertion. Iran has gone out of her way to impress both local and outside powers with her ambitions and her potential for realizing them. Iran's success in its role as caretaker of the Persian Gulf ultimately hinges not only on its own strength, but on its ability to convince the United States and the USSR that the continued assertion of its power is necessary to preserve regional stability.

The Shah operates through informal meetings, personal cliques, and trusted groupings of friends and family. Rivalry and tension are omnipresent. As a result, no one becomes too powerful and the leader remains far above any potential challenger. In Iran, the network of balanced rivalry encompasses the royal family, courtiers, personal adjutants, ministers, military generals, and all economic and political personalities of any important standing. The efficiency of Iranian bureaucracy is therefore partly a function of the degree to which the Shah is capable of dealing adequately with all the parallel lines of administration. Finally, the Shah of Iran has always sought to maintain a special and direct control over the military. As commander in chief, the Shah selects military leaders primarily on the basis of their loyalty to him. The Shah's immediate circle of advisers is also surprisingly small. Among them are Premier Amir Abbas Hoveida, 54; Hushang Ansary, 46, minister of economic affairs and finance; Amir Assadullah Alam, 55, who acts as the sovereigns's right hand as minister of the Imperial Court; Jamshid Amuzegar, 51, representative to OPEC and minister of the Interior. Although, they are unswervingly loyal, it is frequently suggested that the Shah's ministers insulate him from affairs. This may often preclude debate on important decisions.

Outputs

Iran is the only Persian Gulf state present at the 1958 and 1960 Geneva Conferences as well as the Hague Conference of 1930. Iran is the only state in the region that has signed the four conventions which emerged from the 1958 Geneva Conference. Although Iran has not ratified these conventions, she has to a large extent used the principles contained therein.

Iran was the first Persian Gulf state to define its territorial sea. By a law of July 19, 1934, it extended its sovereignty to a belt of sea 6 nautical miles from the low-water mark with an additional 6 miles of contiguous zone.[74] This was consistent with the position taken by the Persian delegation at the Hague Conference of 1930 and the regional precedents set by the Ottoman Empire in 1914. In 1959 Iran extended its territorial sea to 12 nautical miles. Iran has also favored the establishment of a contiguous zone beyond the territorial sea limit.

Iran, together with 13 other Afro-Asian and Latin American countries, co-sponsored a document submitted to the Caracas session of the United Nations Law of the Sea Conference, according to which the powers and controls recognized under Article 24 of the 1958 Convention on the Territorial Sea and Contiguous Zone may be exercised by the coastal state in an area within the economic zone beyond the territorial sea.[75] Underlying Iranian thinking on the question of territorial sea is the contention that the 12-mile limit should not be interpreted in such a way as to exclude the possibility of bilateral or multilateral agreements in cases where special circumstances exist. Iran also sympathizes with the view of the archipelagic states that their territorial sea should be generally limited by rationally established baselines. However, beyond those lines, Iran contends that foreign vessels sailing in established corridors must be guaranteed right of passage within those baselines.[76]

There appears to be a consensus that a 12-mile territorial sea linked with a 188-mile economic zone beyond the territorial sea will emerge from the Third U.N. Law of the Sea Conference. However, Iran sees two principal problems with such a zone. One relates to the passage of foreign ships through the straits used for international navigation, which are less than 24 nautical miles wide; the other concerns the regime of the economic zone. As to the first, the problem is that most of the major maritime powers, particularly the United States and the Soviet Union, have insisted that the extension of the territorial sea to 12 miles should not interfere with the freedom of passage through the straits used for international navigation. However, states bordering the straits have, for security or environmental reasons, resisted the notion of free transit or free passage by foreign ships through waters they consider part of their territorial sea. Iran, therefore, relies on the concept of innocent passage and the indivisibility of the territorial sea.

The Strait of Hormuz lies between Iran on the north and north-west and Oman on the south. The narrowest part of the Strait is 20¾ miles wide at the northeastern end between Larak Island off the Iranian coast and the Great Quoin Island off the coast of Oman. Iran and Oman have both claimed 12-mile territorial seas. Moreover, they have both drawn straight baselines for the measurement of their territorial seas in the Strait of Hormuz and elsewhere. The territorial seas of the two countries overlap for a distance of 13 miles along the strait. In the Iranian view, this should not pose any legal problem for the passing of ships exercising the right of innocent passage. But the configuration of the strait (whose navigable channels run close to the coast and through half a dozen Iranian or Omani islands) puts the two strait states in a hazardous position. Iran asserts that the security and pollution risks are tremendous. The strait leads to the world's richest oil fields; maritime traffic is extremely heavy in the Gulf. At the Caracas session of the conference, Iran stressed the point that the sovereignty of the coastal state in its territorial sea is subject only to the exercise of the right of innocent passage of foreign ships and that a strait situated within the territorial sea should be considered as a part of the territorial sea. Iran emphasizes however that objective rules could be established to safeguard the passage of foreign ships through the straits while adequately accommodating the security and environmental interests of the coastal state.[77] Iran recognizes the vital importance of the exclusive economic zone for the coastal states, but feels that a just solution must be found for the limits of the zone to enable the developing countries, particularly the landlocked ones, to enjoy the benefits of the exploitation of resources.[78]

The establishment of an economic zone of 200 miles is most advantageous to states that border open oceans. It is far less beneficial to states facing narrow or enclosed seas. Aside from the landlocked states, the least privileged countries will be those that either have short coastlines or border narrow or enclosed seas. With the exception of Oman, all the Persian Gulf states fall into the so-called geographically disadvantaged category.

On the basis of the 1958 Convention and of the special geographical and geological situation in the Persian Gulf, Iran has already reached agreement with several states as to the delimitation of the continental shelf. In the division of their seabed areas the Gulf states have been guided by the following principles: resort to agreement as opposed to arbitration or judicial settlement of dispute; the use of equidistance criterion as a guide and point of departure rather than as a principle; and the division of the seabed and its subsoil resources in accordance with equitable principles.

Although Iran considers the 12-mile limit suitable for establishing the extent of the territorial sea, it considers it inadequate for guaranteeing the protection of the vital fishery interests. Fishing fleets are now able to come from distant regions and endanger many species of fish as well as the fishing industry of Iran. Aware of the danger of the exhaustion of certain species in its coastal waters and to protect its fishing industry, Iran by the Proclamation of October 30, 1973 claimed an exclusive fishery zone on the Persian Gulf and the Sea of Oman.[79] The proclamation was based on the historical rights of the inhabitants of the coasts of Iran and on the importance of the natural resources of the sea for the economic and social development of the country. The statement makes it clear that the fishing zone includes that part of the continental shelf belonging to Iran under existing agreements on the division of the continental shelf, and a median line will be enforced between Iran and those states with which no formal agreement exists. In the Sea of Oman the fishing area is defined by a line drawn 50 miles from the Iranian baseline. The move, although officially based on conservation is a further sign of Iranian assertiveness and a demonstration of its naval ability to control movements in the area. Iran advocates as "a next step" the establishment of a regional fishing commission to ensure the rational use of the coastal waters of the countries of the region.

Iran notes that the 1973 International Convention for the Prevention of Pollution from Ships defines the Persian Gulf and the Sea of Oman as a special zone requiring additional precautions for the protection of the marine environment. Until that convention takes effect, Iran's internal regulations are applied up to the limits of the superjacent waters of the continental shelf. However, Iran considers this insufficient, since there are no limits to pollution. Accordingly, international and regional agreements take on a vital importance for Iran. Using the Helsinki Convention as a model of regional agreement, Iran has fully supported the invitation of the Kuwaiti government to the Persian Gulf states to hold a conference to develop regional solutions to the pollution problem. Iran maintains that, in the struggle against pollution caused in particular by oil tankers and other merchant vessels, standards should be laid down by an international authority to avoid multiplicity of regulations. Iran envisioned IMCO playing an important role in this regard.[80]

Iran steadfastly maintains throughout its various positions on the law of the sea that the geographical configuration, the socioeconomic setting, and the vulnerability of a small body of water such as the Persian Gulf demand special treatment. Global norms may not necessarily be adequate for those areas. Iran strongly advocates global standards supplemented by regional standards that take into account the economic, environmental, and security interests of the littoral states.[81]

A truly effective armed force in the Persian Gulf requires a credible navy. In this regard, Iran has placed much emphasis on developing a naval capability. Today it is the major naval force in the Gulf possessing a significant offensive potential and a Gulf-wide quick-reaction capability. Indeed Iran's operational hovercraft fleet, reportedly the most extensive of its type in the world, is slated for further expansion.[82] In addition, Iran is approaching the point where she will control seaborne traffic in the Gulf. From new naval gun emplacements on Abu

Musa and the Greater Tunb Islands, the Iranians are making spot radio checks of transiting vessels.[83]

The extent of Iran's maritime buildup is emphasized by the fact that Teheran's naval presence is not limited to the Persian Gulf. Confident of his control over the Persian Gulf, the Shah has indicated his intention to extend Iran's presence to the Indian Ocean to counter growing Soviet naval strength. Iran's concern is two-fold. It views the Indian Ocean as an extension of Persian Gulf oil lanes. To anchor her Indian Ocean defenses, on the southwestern coast of Iran at Chah Bahar, a $600 million army, navy, and air force base is being constructed. Reportedly, this will be the largest base of its kind anywhere in the Indian Ocean.[84] Iran is also reported to have agreed to give Mauritius substantial aid for the right to use its port facilities.[85] Iran has developed a relatively powerful navy and has provided it with adequate air cover. As a result, it is unlikely that any other Gulf littoral state could effectively challenge Iranian naval power.

Conclusions

Iran's drive for control of shipping in the Gulf, through which two-thirds of the non-Communist world's oil imports pass, tends to conflict with the tenets of free navigation that the United States and other maritime powers would like to see incorporated in a law of the sea treaty. In March 1973 Iran was reported to be exploring an agreement with Oman to inspect all ships passing through the Straits of Hormuz.[86] Observers of Gulf politics regarded Iran's announced concern about the threat of pollution as secondary to its concern about Arab governments' supplying arms to radicals. Iran's inclination to seek control of shipping in the Gulf may run counter to an ideal global law of the sea treaty; but, considering the more than $2 billion in arms the United States has provided Iran to bolster its claim to paramountcy in the Gulf, Iran's foreign policy may not be inconsistent with America's broad security interests in the Gulf.[87]

Oil is the mainstay and the principal commodity of the countries around the Gulf. The national economies of almost all of them are heavily dependent upon oil. An endless armada of tankers thread the narrow throat of the Persian Gulf. It is estimated that the rate of passage through the Strait of Hormuz averages one loaded tanker every ninety minutes, with cargoes totaling 600 million tons of oil a year.[88] Few of the Gulf states can be economically viable without oil unless they diversify their economies. The diversification process has begun and is gaining momentum.

Accordingly, the sum of Iran's maritime perspective has intensified in all aspects. To achieve a new and comprehensive legal order for the uses of the sea, Iran brings a flexible and openminded attitude to deliberations. In general terms, Iran proposes that:

1. The priority interests of the coastal state in all marine activities adjacent to its shores must be appropriately recognized and reflected in international law.
2. Much of the administration of the law of the future must be based on resource and environmental management concepts.
3. For any agreement to endure, there must be a better balance between the rights of individual states, whether flag or coastal, and the responsibilities these rights carry with them regarding vital community interests in the uses of the sea.

As a developing country, with a major stake in all issues pertaining to marine affairs, Iran has a continuing interest in all conferences touching on the management and preservation of ocean resources.

The Case of Nigeria

Background and Inputs

Nigeria represents an interesting case study as a recently independent (1960) African nation. Like many developing nations, Nigeria has had to confront enormous problems that, if not solved, would undermine any chances for economic and political development. Marine matters in Nigeria must compete for attention; numerous other issue areas—political and economic—all detract from a marine focus, especially since Nigeria traditionally has not been a sea-faring nation and until recently had neither the economic means nor the desire to pursue and develop marine resources.

Nigeria, the largest coastal state in west Africa, gained independence from the United Kingdom in October 1960 and became a relatively loose federation of three unequal regions.[89] Three years later, it became a republic within the British Commonwealth. It is the most populous country in Africa possessing many natural resources and a varied climate and has an exceptionally broad agricultural base.

Preparation for independence was gradual and included a series of constitutional reforms that gave Nigerian leaders broad experience in self-government and fostered development of a competent corps of civil servants. The federal system adopted by the Nigerians reinforced the tribally oriented regionalism the British used to facilitate indirect rule. Independence did little to change the life-style and the outlook of the average Nigerian citizen.[90] Nigeria, like many states, is a somewhat artificial creation of the colonial period, resulting in borders that include highly diverse people, divided by language, culture, religion and tribal allegiances. The first principal political subdivisions of the new country reflected the influence of major ethnic groups and largely ignored the interests of the lesser minorities. An undercurrent of ethnic antagonism developed and was intensified by the central government's domination by a single group and by regional differences in economic development.

After five years of multiparty democracy, pressures to unite Nigeria precipitated a coup that brought General Ironsi to power. Due to tribal rivalries, Ironsi's efforts failed. In 1966 Lieutenant Colonel Yakubu Gowon, a less controversial figure, assumed power. Gowon's efforts to make the government more responsive and to end the monopoly of political power and patronage enjoyed by the major tribes were begun by dividing Nigeria into 12 states. The effort failed resulting in the secession of the eastern region and civil war.

The two- and one-half-year war ended with the usual problems of reconstruction, relief, and reconciliation but seemed to produce greater national unity and resolve.[91] The conflict spurred the development of the petroleum and manufacturing industries, thus generating the capital needed to attack other economic problems. The need for assistance during the conflict forced Nigeria from an isolationist position and created a new image as an active and influential member of the group of nonaligned nations. This, along with active participation in African affairs, contributed to the growth of Nigerian nationalism.

To put it mildly, the recent political situation in Nigeria has been volatile. Unexpectedly, General Gowon was overthrown in a coup on July 29, 1975.[92] The principal reasons for the coup seem to have been the indecision and inactivity of the Gowon regime.[93] The new head of state, Brigadier Murtala Ramat Mohammed, seemed to enjoy some measure of success until he was killed in an attempted coup on February 13, 1976.[94] Although it is too early to predict his ultimate success, the new leader, Lieutenant-General Olusegun Obasanjo, appears to be the best qualified of Nigeria's recent strongmen.[95]

Nigeria is composed of diverse physical, sociological, and economic zones. The tropical climate is modulated by temperature, humidity, and rainfall from the northern reaches to the southern extent of the country. Northern geography fostered the development of pastoral pursuits, caravan trade, and large but loosely knit empires dependent on cavalry to police the domains. Due to trade development to the north, the Nigerians were heavily influenced by the Arab culture. The Nigerians themselves come from tribal groups divided more by language, culture, and history, than by physical characteristics. Some two hundred and fifty tribes and an equal number of dialects have been identified. There is still no single language understood throughout Nigeria, although English is the official language.

Agriculture is still the backbone of the Nigerian economy. Although no longer the principal source of export earnings, agricultural pursuits account for nearly half of the country's gross domestic product (GDP) and employ nearly 70 percent of the labor force. With less than half of the arable land under cultivation, Nigeria is nearly self-sufficient in food and agricultural raw materials.

Although agricultural production has increased slowly, mining and manufacturing have been growing very rapidly. Nigeria is the only West African country that has all forms of primary energy in excess of internal consumption requirements. Commercial quantities of oil were discovered in 1956. By mid-1972 Nigeria ranked eighth among the world's oil producing nations with a daily output of about 1.8 million barrels. By the end of 1971, net foreign exchange had risen to over 1 billion dollars. The contribution of oil to the government revenues increased from $38 million, or 9 percent of the total revenue in 1966 to $983 million or well over one-half of the total revenues in 1971.[96]

Although revenue from oil resources is significant, it is not a panacea. Nigeria's oil resources are not as extensive as those of Middle Eastern states whose populations are much smaller. The oil industry still tends not to employ Nigerians in many top management positions. Growth prospects for Nigeria as a whole will depend equally on achievements outside the oil sector and on the efficiency with which the government revenues are disbursed to meet federal and state requirements.

Processing

With a very large population and substantial need for protein, Nigeria is turning toward the oceans. As one of the largest and most populous countries in Africa, Nigeria views itself as a leader in African affairs. Examining the trends in marine policy for Nigeria might be indicative of the policies adopted by other African nations.

The Federal Republic of Nigeria has been ruled by decree since January 1966, when a small group of military officers ousted the civilian government and suspended the complex system of federal and regional executives and the parliament. In May 1966 the military government replaced the federal system with a unitary one; however, another military coup reinstated the federation. In 1968 the four regions that had constituted the federation were replaced by a twelve-state system.[97] The government is run by the military with the aid of civil servants. The head of the Federal Military Government (FMG) announces government decrees formulated by him with a small group of advisors and confirmed by the military hierarchy. The head of the Federal Military Government, until the recent coup, was General Gowon.[98] He made progress in building a constituency among the various tribes. Gowon used the expertise of the predominantly civilian Federal Executive Council. Key decisions were made either by Gowon himself with the help of unofficial advisors or were left to senior civil servants.

All executive and legislative power is vested in the Federal Military Government. Laws are made and implemented through decrees signed by the head of the FMG, who is also commander in chief of the armed forces and chairman of the Federal Executive Council (FEC). The absolute supremacy of the military government was publicly asserted in a 1970 decree that abolished judicial review of governmental decisions.[99]

During the Gowon era policy making was carried out by a relatively institutionalized group of top military and political advisors. The membership of the Supreme Military Council (SMC) includes: the head of the FMG; the governors of the twelve states; the heads of the army, navy, and air force; the chief of staff of Supreme Headquarters; the commandant of the Nigerian Defense Academy; the naval officer in command, Lagos Command; former army chief of staff Major General Kalsuia; and the two top police officials. Proposals formally approved by the SMC are already debated by the same persons acting in their unofficial capacity as advisors to the head of state.[100]

In addition to the ministries there are a number of statutory corporations of importance in the administration of the government and the economy. They include the Nigerian Railway Corporation, the Electricity Corporation of Nigeria, and the Port Authority. A new body of potential significance is the Nigerian National Oil Corporation.[101]

Nigeria's twelve-state federal structure is designed to achieve a balance of power between the central government and the diverse regional interests.[102] The federal government has exclusive power over such matters as defense, foreign affairs, and interregional and foreign trade and commerce. The federal and regional governments have concurrent power over labor affairs, public order, industrial development, and public works; in cases of conflict, federal authority prevails.[103] Regions hold exclusive power in such fields as education, health, and agriculture. However, the influence of the FMG is extended throughout the regions through the appointment of all of the governors. Of course any analysis of Nigeria's governmental processes must contend with the fact that there have been recent violent changes in the personnel of that government. After the coup that overthrew General Gowon in July 1975, General Mohammed became head of state. When General Mohammed was assassinated on February 13, 1976, Lieutenant-General Olusegun Obasanjo came to power.[104] Although it is still early, it appears that the basic power arrangements are unchanged. Certain long-awaited reforms, for example, the drafting of a new constitution, appear to be progressing on schedule.[105] The fact that Obasanjo has vast experience in many aspects of foreign and domestic policy and is well respected perhaps portends a better future.[106]

It is official government policy to promote greater economic participation by Nigerians in the economy. The "Nigerianization" decree reserves 22 small-scale manufacturing and service fields for Nigerians and requires at least 40 percent Nigerian ownership of certain important industries. However, only a small part of the total foreign investment is affected, although government involvement in the petroleum industry has been substantial.[107]

Fisheries regulated by the Agricultural Ministry contribute less than 5 percent of the GDP. Expansion has been hindered by the lack of satisfactory fishing terminals, trained manpower, and suitable fishing vessels. The federal government has entered into industrial fishing operations so, after long neglect, the fishing industry is assuming some importance.[108]

The federal government has recently waived the 15 percent value-added tax on the wholesale price of fish landed by Nigerians as well as the 25 percent tax on foreign-owned vessels as a means of increasing production. Perhaps the proposal made by the National Fisheries Development Committee, which called for the removal of tax on fuel used in fishing and for the exemption of imported fisheries equipment from duty, may be enstated as well.[109]

As some of the states and the federal government begin marine industrial fisheries, operating costs will be high because of the slow development and competition from other countries. Eventually Nigeria may resort to legislation that will restrict foreign vessels to protect against losses. At this time neither the state nor federal government considers fisheries a big enough industry to warrant the creation of a separate ministry.[110]

Energy resources, especially petroleum, are an important element in Nigerian policy making. In July 1971 Nigeria became the eleventh member of the Organization of Petroleum Exporting Countries (OPEC).[111] Nigeria has one petroleum refinery (55,000 barrels a day capacity) that barely meets the domestic need for refined petroleum products. Nigeria became a leading producer in the late 1960s; current production is the largest on the African continent. Nigerian reserves are also substantial, including three giant natural-gas fields as well as petroleum. Nigeria has indicated some willingness to make modest price concessions to her African neighbors, but OPEC's objection has been strenuous. Recently Nigeria \reduced production to about 2 million barrels a day; although the reason given was conservation, the deteriorating market for premium-priced oil also may have been a factor.[112]

Nigerian national policies since independence have been expressed in two main goals: national unity and economic development. In economic development, the income from oil production has balanced the federal budget and provided foreign exchange. Directly after the civil war the cost of reconstruction absorbed much of the national budget. The government is endeavoring to secure full employment and to place effective control of all of the major industries in Nigerian hands. Marine-related industries are prime targets for the nationalization process. In the petroleum industry the Nigerian government has moved to acquire 55 percent control of foreign concessions.[113] Fishing industry licensing may be withheld from the newly discovered shrimping grounds for those ships that are not partly owned by Nigerians.

Policy making in Nigeria usually begins with the ministry that is involved preparing a memorandum, which is then sent to the Federal Executive Council through the commissioner of the ministry. The FEC decides if legislation on the matter should be prepared. The task of preparing draft legislation falls to the Federal Ministry of Justice, which works closely with the ministry. If agreement is reached, the final draft is sent to the FEC for approval and on to the Supreme Military Council for ratification. The head of state and commander-in-chief of the armed forces formally promulgates the law. The principal statute normally gives the commissioner in charge of the ministry concerned the power to promulgate regulations. Once approved, the commissioner signs the regulations and they thereby become effective.[114]

Nigeria's size and location predispose an intense interest in all West African affairs. Nigeria, as a result of size, population, and military strength, is the principal leader of the West African bloc. Nigeria was instrumental in the formation of the Organization of African Unity. Although favorably disposed to the West, the Nigerian government is pursuing a nonaligned policy.[115] The policy has been evolving continually as the FMG's standing in Africa has been enhanced. Relations with other African states have been excellent; one of the top foreign policy priorities has been coordinated economic development and regional unity in West Africa. Nigerian nonalignment is a pragmatic policy allowing decisions to be made on the merits of issues while maintaining flexibility. By necessity Nigeria's foreign policy decisions have been compromises between traditional ties with Britain and other Western countries and the desire to establish a "Nigerian" identity.[116] Nigeria seems to be trying to reduce her dependence on foreign powers while strengthening economic cooperation within western Africa. There is a great sense of cooperation with those who supported Nigeria during the civil war.[117]

Outputs and Conclusions

Nigeria is party to the 1958 Convention on the High Seas, the 1958 Convention on the Territorial Sea and Contiguous Zone, and the 1948 Convention on the Inter-Governmental Maritime Consultative Organization (IMCO). Nigeria is also a party to the SOLAS Conventions of 1948 and 1960; Prevention of Collision at Sea 1960; Oil Pollution of 1954 and 1962, as well as Facilitation of Maritime Traffic of 1965 and the Load Limit agreement of 1966. Nigeria has been a leader in the Organization of African Unity and a member of the Committee for East Central Atlantic Fisheries (CECAF). During the Third U.N. Conference on the Law of the Sea, Nigeria advocated an exclusive economic zone with absolute rights to explore and exploit the renewable living and nonliving resources of the sea and of the seabed. In 1971 the federal government extended the territorial waters to 30 nautical miles. Also in 1971, the Sea Fisheries Decree established controls over the operation or navigation of motor fishing boats within the territorial waters of Nigeria.[118] The powers of control were vested in the director of the Federal Department of Fisheries, who is the licensing officer, and the federal commissioner charged with the responsibility for fisheries who may make fishing regulations. The 1971 decree also transferred jurisdiction over sea fisheries from the regional or state government to the federal government. Nigeria as a party to the 1958 Geneva Convention on the Territorial Sea and Contiguous Zone sees no conflict between that convention and the decree. The act extending the territorial sea was motivated by reasons of security and economics.

The Petroleum Decree of 1969 Section 1(1) vests the entire ownership and control of all petroleum in, under, or upon and lands to which this section applies to "all lands [including land covered by water] which (a) is in Nigeria, or (b) is under the territorial waters of Nigeria, or (c) forms part of the continental shelf."[119] The revenue derived from oil operations in these areas will go exclusively to the federal government. Since only 5 of the 12 states of the federation have sea coasts to which the Nigerian territorial waters and continental-shelf area are contiguous, it would be unfair to regard the offshore areas as part of these states and to give them preferential treatment in the use and sharing of the resources.[120]

Nigeria, probably like most developing countries, has enormous problems attendant to national development, many of which have no direct bearing on marine policy. Generally, when marine concerns enter the picture it is because they relate directly to problems of national development, for example, petroleum and fishing. Like most developing countries, Nigeria has few marine concerns that extend beyond her immediate coastal region. It seems that with many pressing problems, among them rebuilding after the civil war, Nigeria cannot be expected to have a concerted approach to marine problems. In fact, it may be perfectly reasonable that no such approach exists. When one considers the urgent goals enumerated by President Gowon in 1970,[121] it is little wonder that marine concerns can be little more than means to more fundamental ends.

The Case of the Philippines

Background and Inputs

The Republic of the Philippines is an archipelago consisting of 7,107 islands extending about "1,100 miles north to south along the southeastern rim of Asia."[122] By virtue of its archipelagic composition, the Philippines claims internal control over its straits, the most important of which are Mindanao, Surigao, and San Bernadino. Eleven of the islands contain roughly 95 percent of the nation's total population and land area.[123] The Philippines, due to its archipelagic status, has an extensive coastline with many natural ports and harbors and countless navigable gulfs and bays.[124] The Philippines has 184,600 square kilometers of continental shelf within 200 miles of its coast.[125]

The earliest settlement of the Philippines was some 30,000 years ago, most likely by means of land bridges then existing from Borneo and Sumatra. These first people were the Negritoes. Eventually, settlers of Malay stock, arriving by way of the land bridges and later by small boats, became dominant. A social system based upon family relationships, widespread by the sixteenth century, remains intact today. In 1521 Ferdinand Magellan discovered the Philippine Islands and claimed them for Spain. The nation remained under Spanish rule for 377 years. The Spanish organized the Philippines along their colonial system with a strong centralized government and a highly structured bureaucracy. The wealthier and more educated Filipinos were employed at the local level in this bureaucracy. For 250 years, galleon trade between the islands and Spain and its colonies flourished. These ships, of approximately 1,000 tons, were built in the Philippines from native hardwood.[126] Chinese immigrants were attracted by this trade and soon outnumbered the Spanish in Manila.[127] .

The Jones Act of 1916 gave Philippine control to the country's legislature. A judicial system and the civil service, which flourished as a result of historical precedent, were developed. The Tyding-McDuffie Act of 1935 made the Philippines a self-governing commonwealth with independence to be granted within ten years. The outbreak of World War II intervened with Japanese occupation continuing until 1945. In spite of wartime damage, the United States granted independence to the Philippines on July 4, 1946.

The Filipinos have an "outward seeking mentality of a seafaring people."[129] Their Malay forefathers arrived at the islands by boat. For almost 300 years, the Philippine islands were the "way-station between the Orient and Spain and Mexico."[130]

The many islands closely grouped together and separated by calm seas have made the Filipinos water-oriented people. Commerce and everyday communication make extensive use of inexpensive water transport. Roads and railroads do not connect the islands and are secondary to water transport in importance. Dependence on waterways has profoundly influenced the settlement patterns on the islands. Most communities were originally established in narrow bands along the seashore or on rivers and streams.[131]

With its many fine harbors, the Philippine Republic has an excellent present and potential sea trade. Fishing is also an important marine resource, both as a source of protein and income. Since the people view the ocean as important, the Philippine government can be expected to take an active interest in marine matters. In 1973 Philippine sea trade amounted to 29,000 tons. Although sea trade is already important to the Philippines, it has even greater potential. Philippine flag vessels carry only 10 percent of the nation's overseas trade. In 1973 only 154 vessels composed the country's maritime fleet; 11 of these were over 10,000 gross tons, with 44 in the 5,000–10,000 gross tons classification.[132] China and the USSR have entered the area of Philippine sea trade. Filsov Shipping Company, a Soviet concern, is undercharging the other shipping lines serving the Philippines.

A recent 26 percent rate increase by the conference lines prompted the Philippines to join Indonesia, Malaysia, Singapore, and Thailand in calling an Association of Asian Nations' Conference in an attempt to reduce the hold of the major shipping concerns such as the Far East Freight Conference.

The Port of Manila is being enlarged and modernized, and another port is being planned for Batangas approximately 100 miles away.[133] The government's shipping plan includes:

. . . the maximum use of shipyards for dry-docking and repairs [encouragement of manufacturing in a number of related industries, upgrading] of engineering standards and production skills and [to] provide technological expertise for the industry in general.[134]

The newly created Maritime Industry Authority will implement this program.

In September 1973, the Philippine government signed the largest service contract it had ever made with an international oil conglomerate.[135] Within a week, this corporation brought in a drilling rig for offshore oil exploration in the Sulu Sea area adjacent to a successful oil venture off the northern coast of Borneo. Special incentives are offered in the form of tax exemptions to foreign investors interested in offshore oil exploration. Although oil has, as yet, not been discovered in the Sulu Sea, experts agree that it certainly will be. One writer has stated that "the most significant motive behind the Muslim struggle, on a regionwide basis, is the potential for oil under the Sulu Sea."[136] Although this statement may be an exaggeration, the potential for offshore oil surely figures highly in the factors prompting the conflict.

Fishing is an important industry in the Philippines, accounting for almost 4 percent of the GNP and employing about 799,000 people.[137] A per-capita fish consumption of 29 kilograms per year is more than twice the world's average; fish provides 54 percent of total supplies of animal protein in the Philippines.[138]

In 1973 the total catch was 1,148,700 metric tons, a sizeable portion of which consists of inland fisheries and fishpond culture.

The national fishery is broadly classified into 1) the marine fishery, which is further divided into commercial and municipal (or sustenance fisheries), 2) fishpond culture and 3) the inland fishery. The subdivision of the marine fishery is on an administrative basis whereby all vessels over 3 tons are licensed by the Philippine Bureau of Fisheries while those of 3 tons and under can fish in municipal waters, which include marine waters up to three miles distant from the coastline.[139]

Distant-water fishing is presently negligible, although the government has recently begun an effort to develop this area as well as all other areas of the fisheries. The offshore waters of the archipelago will soon be developed in spite of the fact that the narrow continental shelves, a lack of unwelling, and a non-mixing wind pattern inhibit the productivity of many areas.

In 1972 President Marcos issued Presidential Decree #43, The Fishery Industry Development Decree of 1972, a basic law designed to promote both inland and marine fisheries. The fishing industry was declared a Board of Investments Pioneer Project providing special investment benefits. The state policy was proclaimed "to accelerate the integrated development of the fishery resources of the country" and "to promote the expansion of fishing effort in international waters."[140] The fishing industry, already an impressive sector of the Philippine economy, will increase in importance. Philippine marine policy will certainly be formulated to protect and promote its fishery resources.

Processing

On September 21, 1972 President Ferdinand Marcos placed the Philippines under martial law. Article VII, Section 10, paragraph 2, of the 1946 Constitution gave him the authority to do so. The right of habeus corpus and all civil liberties were suspended; as commander-in-chief of the armed forces, President Marcos took full control of the government.[141]

President Marcos, as the authoritarian head of the government, has the final word on all governmental decisions, marine and otherwise. All decisions are issued in the form of presidential decrees. Marcos is advised, however, by five of his cabinet members, referred to as the "technocrats." These men are "predominantly young Harvard trained educators serving on the faculty of the University of the Philippines."[142] They are: Cesar Virata, the secretary of finance; Gerardo Sicat, director of the National Economic Development Administration; Juan Eurile, head of the Department of Defense; Vincente Paterno, director of the Board of Administration; Juan Eurile, head of the Department of Defense; Vincente Paterno, director of the Board of Investments; and Francisco Tatad, secretary of Public Information.[143]

The Fisheries Industry Development Council was conceived by the government "to provide the initiative and focus for the Fisheries Development Program."[144] The secretary of Agriculture and Natural Resources is the chairman, and the vice-president and chief executive officer is the director of the Bureau of Fisheries. Council members are: the secretary of National Defense, the governor of the Philippine National Bank, the governor of the Central Bank of the Philippines, the chairman of the Board of Investments and the heads of two fishermen's groups. Originally conceived as a policy-making body, it has since become an advisory and coordinating unit. The council strives:

to provide overall policy guidance, to create a healthy investment climate, and to draw up a comprehensive financial program for the development of fishing industry, and to promote and encourage the development of a modern fishing fleet, infrastructure facilities and improved systems and practices of operation,

and is

an excellent forum for all interested agencies and the private sector to participate in the development of the fishing industry.[145]

The Bureau of Fisheries is the executive unit of the Fisheries Industry Development Council. The bureau makes regulations for fishery management and conservation. Vessels of over three tons are under its licensing and inspection powers. The gathering of fishing statistics, with a view toward future development and management, is also one of its functions. Establishment of fisheries cooperatives and associations and advising them are concerns of the bureau. Fish and fish-products processing are also regulated by the Bureau of Fisheries.[146]

The Maritime Industry Authority was created by President Marcos in 1974 and assigned the task of drawing up a ten-year development plan for the Philippine shipping industry. Still in the initial stages of development, the authority has thus far been concerned mainly with improvement of existing port facilities. However, the Philippine government has stated its intention to develop the areas of shipping and shipbuilding as well. There are four Philippine shipping lines and thirty-seven foreign lines serving the nation. There are sixty operating ports in the islands.[147] The Philippines' position astride many important ocean routes, coupled with its own impressive shipping potential, will certainly bring about the future expansion and prominence of the authority.

Outputs

The major output for the Philippines is that of marine territorial claims. The nation's island composition has resulted in a declaration of archipelagic status.

Many other marine outputs are influenced by this factor. The archipelagic claim of the Philippines has two facets: "extensive historic claims to territorial waters far beyond its shores, and claims to expansive authority over waters more or less between its islands."[148] When Spain ceded the Philippines to the United States in the 1898 Treaty of Paris, the wording of the agreement referred to the islands as an archipelago. This distinction was again reiterated by the Treaty of 1900 between Spain and the United States which spelled out extensive maritime limits.

On March 7, 1955 a note verbale from the delegation of the Philippines to the United Nations stated that all the waters around the Philippine archipelago were "necessary appurtenances of its island territory, forming an integral part of the national or inland waters, subject to the exclusive sovereignty of the Philippines."[149] This statement was reconfirmed in another note verbale on January 20, 1956, and "pursuant to [this claim] the territorial sea is measured from straight baselines connecting the islands of the Archipelago."[150]

In 1961 the Philippine government implemented these provisions by the Act to Define the Baselines of the Territorial Sea of the Philippines:

The waters between the baselines and the . . . 'Treaty Limits' . . . are considered territorial sea. While baseline and treaty limits virtually coincide in the southwest, in the northwest they are separated by approximately 285 nautical miles of the sea.[151]

Thus the territorial sea claim of the Philippines may conflict with certain aspects of current international law.

The Philippines is party to none of the four 1958 Geneva Conventions. In both 1958 and 1960, Indonesia put forth the archipelagic concept at Geneva with support from the Philippines. Too revolutionary a concept at that time, it received active support from only Yugoslavia and Denmark.[152] Since then, however, several states have made similar claims, for example, Ecuador, Iceland, the Faroe Islands, Fiji, and Mauritius. Expected to follow suit are Nauru, Tonga, Western Samoa, the Cook Islands, and the Bahamas.[153] Canada's recent declaration of archipelagic status for its Arctic Islands has added to the ranks.

The Philippines has presented several draft articles dealing with the archipelagic issue. In those articles relating to the territorial sea, it is held that any maximum limit placed on the territorial sea will not apply to historic waters, thus protecting its treaty limits.[154] Of particular controversy are the statements on archipelagoes, specifically those dealing with national jurisdiction over straits within archipelagic waters. Fiji, Indonesia, Mauritius, and the Philippines have stated that the coastal state has sole jurisdiction over straits within its boundaries. Innocent passage, subject to coastal state control, is to be the rule.[155]

The Philippines are situated among important strategic ocean routes. Possible capture and blockade of the straits along these lanes by one of many belligerent forces would seriously hinder the other belligerents by necessitating lengthy detours. Deterrence by means of maximum naval mobility, the component of the superpower naval strategies of utmost importance, would be destroyed. Possession of the straits by foreign powers would, however, seriously disrupt internal communication between the islands of the strait nation.[156] There has been no instance yet in which the Philippines has asserted this claim. It is highly doubtful whether it would be able to enforce the rule. However, as a developing nation striving to achieve a national identity and regional influence, the issue of coastal state control of straits is of political importance and receives attention, particularly from the global naval powers.

In addition, a desire to facilitate communication (largely water-oriented throughout the islands) is served. If a belligerent power were to occupy archipelagic waters, internal security and political neutrality would be jeopardized. Narrow territorial sea limits would also increase the incidence of espionage. Intimidation by naval superpowers would most likely be in the form of proximate maneuvers and demonstrations of naval strength. Control over a wide expanse of territorial sea and passage through it would certainly be of great import to the archipelagic nation.

Control and prevention of ocean-borne pollution resulting from such activities as offshore oil and mineral exploitation, ocean dumping, and tanker transport are of particular interest to an island nation. Pollution of waters leading to coastline fouling or fishery depletion would have serious consequences in the Philippines. Control over the surrounding ocean would have considerable value. In connection with this environmental concern, the Philippines has ratified the 1954 IMCO Oil Pollution Convention.

Conclusions

The Republic of the Philippines is a developing nation with an historical marine orientation and extensive marine resources, both current and potential. The Philippine government is developing and promoting investment in this area. The Philippine archipelago is situated in a politically unstable area. Internal security and communication, political power, and prestige are important goals of this island nation. Although traditionally allied with the United States, and still economically and politically so linked, the Philippines must look to their own existence and success in Southeast Asia.

A developing sense of national identity, combined with economic and political considerations, will figure prominently in the position that the Philippines will take on marine issues. Extensive marine territorial claims and coastal state control over internal straits will remain vital factors to the Philippines. Issues beneficial to fisheries resources and shipping matters will certainly be supported by the archipelagic nation.

Compromises, such as acceptance of a 200-mile economic zone plus a 12-mile territorial sea from the archipelagic baselines, may be unacceptable to the Philippines or accepted only after highly favorable concessions have been made. Exclusive fishing within Philippine waters, whatever the limit, may be dropped in favor of distant water rights when the Philippine fishery expands.

General Conclusions

Certain things are clear from the five case studies. First, and most disappointing, is the difficulty of examining the actual workings of the governments and the way in which marine policy is generated. It was possible to make limited observations about aspects of the processing section and to draw some reasonable inferences. But many of the most important aspects of the marine policy making will remain locked in the inaccessible reaches of national leaders' minds. This seems especially true in the marine area, where usually no single bureaucratic structure exists to handle matters of marine policy. In the absence of a specific structure, it becomes more difficult to trace the policy making process.

Another point that is very clear is that with few exceptions, for example, Canada on pollution, marine concerns are important but not prime or central to the states involved. In most instances, these five countries' marine interests are coastal or at most regional; there is little concern or sympathy with the goals of the maritime powers. It is reasonable to expect that these five are rather typical of most states in the world.

One of the more interesting questions is whether anything in the processing section of the model would so distort the policy-making process that outputs would be totally unexpected given the set of inputs. Four of the five countries have very absolutist rule, where clear decisions can be made with little need to balance divergent views. This may have produced somewhat more definitive policy outputs than might have been expected from the input parameters.

Most of Iran's marine policy must be understood in light of her "manifest destiny" to become the dominant power in the Persian Gulf. Nigeria is so preoccupied with domestic problems that her marine policy can be expected to be pragmatic and resource oriented, tempered mainly by her desire to play a leadership role among African nations. The Philippines, perhaps more than the others, has a long history of strong ties to the oceans. Her archipelagic status produces a unique set of marine concerns that will be afforded the highest priority.

Canada's policy is among the most reasonable given the objective situation. The fragile arctic climate has placed environmental concerns in the forefront. Her legitimate desire to have an independent policy outside the mammoth shadow cast by the United States is also an important factor. The marine posture of

China is affected by organizational factors, specifically the fact that the navy is the weakest part of the military structure and the fact that most of the major leaders in the Communist party come from noncoastal regions. China is patient; she can afford to guard her coastal resources while exercising a broadly defined, antiimperialist position in most areas of marine affairs.

At this point, it is still to be demonstrated if the objective characteristics in the model are sufficient to explain the major aspects of policy without recourse to more detailed analyses of the idiosyncrasies of each state. In the following chapter the issue is confronted when the model is applied. Special attention is paid to these five states, since any policy aberrations glossed over by the model may have been identified in this chapter.

3

General Application of the Model

The task here is to apply the model of marine policy making to the entire world, attempting to discern pattern and regularity. For each state in the world, eighty-nine different characteristics have been tabulated. These characteristics (or attributes or variables) have been chosen according to four principal criteria:

1. Perceived relevance to marine policy
2. Dense coverage, that is, calculable for most states in the world
3. Broad coverage, that is, touching on many different aspects of marine policy
4. Objectivity—characteristics are so-called "hard data" about which there is little disagreement

The emphasis throughout this section is on general patterns. In spite of considerable care in the selection and tabulation of the data, there remains room for error, disagreement, and interpretation. For example, shoreline length, one of the variables, can be measured in many different ways, each of which produces different results. But problems like this can be minimized so long as the measures are consistent, that is, the same technique or method is used for each country. Great care was exercised to ensure consistency. Throughout this section the focus is on the general patterns of the variables and on country groupings, not on the individual attributes of states, although the latter when aggregated determine the former. The reader whose principal interest is individual country positions should consult other sources.[1]

The variables are grouped and numbered according to the role they play in the model. Input variables are designated with an "I" and then numbered sequentially. There are twenty-two input variables, 5 nonmarine and seventeen marine. It should be borne in mind that the inputs all derive from the basic geographic situation of the country; thus nothing resulting from human activity is included as an input. As can be seen from table 3A-1 (appended to this chapter), the input variables attempt to accommodate diverse elements of the basic geographic situation of the countries.

The table provides a complete explanation for each variable, including the source of the information, the average value and standard deviation, and variable values for five countries, that is, the top ranked, the 25th-percentile country, the 50th-percentile country, the 75th-percentile country, and the bottom ranked. The table contains a huge amount of information; one of the problems with this approach to marine policy is the vast amount of specific information. In fact, the principal research task of this section is to find appropriate ways to organize, simplify, interpret, and analyze the information.

It was acknowledged earlier that the processing section of the model can be handled only quickly and superficially when the goal is macroscopic analysis. However, four of the variables in the model have bearing on the ways by which inputs are molded (or distorted) to produce policy outputs. These four are designated P1 through P4 to indicate that they are part of the processing section of the model.

The output section of the model (and the table) is the most important portion; in fact, the other elements have importance only as they relate to the outputs. The output variables have been grouped according to nonmarine and marine characteristics. Nonmarine outputs reflect basic national traits, for example, population, and gross national product, as well as other attributes inferred have probable bearing on marine characteristics, such as several of the variables related to the use of the International Court of Justice and the general issue of dispute settlement. These were thought to be germane, since any new law of the sea treaty will contain important provisions on the settlement of international marine disputes. Several of the group of nonmarine outputs are derived from other variables in the model, for example, scientists per population is a measure of scientific manpower in proportion to the total population of the countries. Although there is some duplicative effect, it is felt that these derivative variables add a certain measure of precision and perhaps parsimony to the model.

The marine output section of the model is of prime importance; an understanding of the interrelationship among marine outputs is the raison d'etre of the whole exercise. The other elements in the model are of interest mainly if they shed light on the set of marine outputs. The marine outputs reflect a wide range of elements comprising a country's marine posture and policy. Certain of the variables are indicative of a state's maritime capacity, for example, shipbuilding and seaborne trade. Others relate directly to naval strength and orientation, that is, coastal versus global naval capacity. Another set of the outputs relates directly to fishing activities of states including fish consumption, imports and exports, and total fish catch. Activities and relationships to certain marine-related international organizations are other outputs. States' relationships to the four 1958 Geneva Conventions as well as the IMCO Oil Pollution Conventions are also part of the output section of the model. These should give some indication of states' propensity to participate in traditional manifestations of the law of the sea. Among the most demonstrative aspects of marine policy are specific claims to marine territory—these are accommodated in territorial sea width and claim to an exclusive fisheries zone. Other claims occur but, at present, these are the dominant ones.

Few of the outputs have direct bearing on the ongoing Third United Nations Law of the Sea Conference. Although this conference will play a dominant role in determining the future course of the law of the sea, it seems premature to deal extensively with material from that conference. Since any new treaty that is adopted by the conference will undoubtedly provide considerable latitude in interpretation and application, it can be expected that many of the tendencies and preferences discovered here will be important as the new legal regime created by the treaty develops. Nevertheless, two variables taken directly from the United Nations Conference are included. The first is the total size of the delegation sent to the conference—this should give an indication of interest in and concern about the oceans. The second conference variable is the stand taken by countries on the issue of the exclusive economic zone. A scale indicates the restrictiveness of the zone advocated by the country. It was felt that this should be included due to the importance that 200-mile zones have played in the conference.

The balance of the outputs are hybrids that relate marine attributes to other national characteristics. These serve the purpose of putting the marine outputs into context, for example, two research vessels may be little marine commitment for a state with a trillion dollar GNP, but they are an enormous commitment for a state with $10 million GNP. With very few exceptions the variables are at least ordinal in nature. This permits the use of more powerful statistical techniques that can reduce the mass of information to more manageable proportions.

Importance of the Processing Section

Before addressing the more general problems of analyzing the interrelationships of the variables, it is instructive to look at the processing section of the model to see what evidence exists that the processing characteristics are associated with certain types of marine-policy outputs. This can be done in two different ways depending upon the nature of the processing variables themselves. Two of the process variables, Years of Independence and Age of Constitution, are interval valued, meaning that correlation coefficients are an appropriate technique to employ. Correlations, like the Pearson's r applied here, indicate the size and direction of the relationship between attributes. Or put another way, they indicate whether large values of one characteristic tend to occur in the same cases (countries) as high values of other characteristics. Correlations can range in value from -1.0 to +1.0. Positive values means that high values on one attribute tend to occur in the same cases as high values in the other variable. For example, land area correlates +.52 with population. This means that those countries with large population also tend to have small areas. Since the value is far from a perfect +1.0, there are many exceptions to the rule, for example, large countries with small populations. Correlations are negative when large values on one variable tend to occur in those cases having small values on the other variable. For example, one would expect GNP per capita to be negatively correlated with infant mortality, since, presumably, as a state becomes wealthier it can provide better health for its people. Correlations are of prime importance throughout this entire section.

Table 3-1 presents all correlations between P3 Years of Independence, P4 Age of Constitution, and any marine-output variables so long as the correlation is at least .35. There are some definite associations—it seems that those states with long independence and old constitutions tend to be more involved in international and global aspects of marine activity, that is, they have large amounts of ocean trade, global navies, and are importers and exporters of fish. But it must be remembered that none of these values is especially large and more important is the fact that 80 percent of the marine output variables did not meet the .35 cutoff criterion. Thus, although some of the individual results may be enlightening, it seems that these two elements of the processing section of the model are not a *major* determinant in marine policy.

Table 3-2 provides the first detailed view of the marine-output variables. Average values on all marine-output variables are given for nine groups of countries

Table 3-1
Correlation Between Processing Characteristics and Marine Outputs

		P3 Years of Independence[a]	P4 Age of Constitution[a]
024	Merchant Shipping Tonnage	–	.38
026	Seaborne Trade	.38	.38
028	Fish Imports	.36	.41
029	Fish Exports	–	.43
032	Fishery Commission Membership	.36	–
033	UN LOS Conference Delegation	.43	.43
035	SCOR Membership	.44	.49
050	Large Naval Vessels Coastal Naval Vessels	.39	.47

Note: Included all correlations greater than + .35 or less than –.35.

[a]The correlation between Years of Independence and Age of Constitution is +.41.

Table 3-2
Means and Standard Deviations of Marine Outputs According to Region and Degree of Political Competition

Marine Outputs	Low Political Competition (n = 52)	Med. Political Competition (n = 64)	High Political Competition (n = 26)	W. Europe & English Speaking (n = 29)	Latin America (n = 24)	USSR & Eastern Europe (n = 9)	Middle East & N. Africa (n = 19)	Sub-Saharan Africa (n = 34)	Southeast Asia (n = 27)
020 Research vessels	2.6(15)	.2(.7)	7.3(16.3)	6.2(15.6)	.2(.8)	13(36)	.4(.9)	.1(.4)	1.0(2.2)
021 Naval vessels (large)	15(67)	3(7)	27(63)	26(60)	5(8)	61(158)	2(4)	.4(1.8)	7.8(14.0)
022 Naval vessels (coastal)	49(107)	10(20)	40(45)	39(41)	12(13)	96(161)	19(25)	3(5)	54(115)
023 Submarines	9(55)	.8(2.4)	11(25)	10(24)	.8(1.6)	46(131)	.7(2.8)	.1(.5)	3.0(8.9)
024 Merchant shipping tonnage (10,000)	80(200)	123(659)	557(926)	467(734)	63(189)	180(338)	274(1,137)	7(28)	163(657)
025 Ship building (1,000)	80(235)	1.4(4.9)	886(2,504)	390(554)	7(26)	285(371)	.9(3.2)	.07(.34)	490(2,472)
026 Seaborne trade (1,000)	19(30)	17(43)	106(140)	79(116)	19(43)	24(38)	50(60)	4.5(10.8)	29(91)
027 Fish catch	579(1,763)	115(329)	857(2,015)	503(799)	532(2,153)	933(2,408)	40(58)	72(191)	779(1,898)
028 Fish imports (100)	94(187)	25(45)	1,014(1,763)	827(1,651)	56(87)	294(329)	11(20)	21(41)	15(56)
029 Fish exports (100)	154(500)	50(122)	633(936)	502(730)	224(692)	142(291)	29(79)	22(78)	19(64)
030 Oil production offshore	2.6(14.6)	1.1(4.8)	3.2(12.7)	2.8(12.1)	.3(.9)	0(0)	8.8(24.3)	.8(4.3)	.3(1.0)
031 Seafood consumption per capita	18.3(20.3)	14.5(17.2)	39.3(30.5)	29.9(27.9)	21.1(22.3)	11.9(10.0)	5.6(7.6)	24.5(17.8)	23.0(28.7)
032 Fisheries commission membership	1.4(1.8)	.7(.8)	3.0(3.5)	2.8(2.9)	.6(.8)	2.3(2.9)	.9(.7)	.7(.7)	1.3(2.4)
033 UN LOS Conference delegation size	9.3(7.6)	6.2(4.8)	21.7(24.1)	20.0(22.6)	8.8(5.4)	13.6(13.5)	7.9(4.0)	4.7(2.5)	8.1(9.4)
034 IOC membership	.60(.50)	.45(.50)	.85(.37)	.76(.44)	.63(.49)	.67(.50)	.63(.50)	.38(.49)	.52(.51)
035 SCOR membership	.40(.91)	.28(.88)	2.62(2.79)	2.34(2.73)	.50(1.14)	.78(1.09)	.16(.69)	.01(.51)	.52(1.12)
036 UN Seabed Committee membership	.60(.50)	.59(.50)	.73(.45)	.72(.45)	.71(.46)	.78(.44)	.58(.51)	.53(.51)	.51(.51)

Table 3-2 – (Continued)

037 1958 Territorial Sea Convention	1.9(1.3)	1.7(1.1)	2.5(1.3)	2.3(1.3)	2.0(1.1)	2.6(1.2)	1.3(.7)	1.7(1.3)	1.9(1.3)
038 1958 Continental Shelf Convention	2.1(1.3)	1.9(1.2)	2.7(1.4)	2.7(1.4)	2.4(1.2)	3.2(1.3)	1.4(.8)	1.8(1.3)	1.9(1.2)
039 1958 High Seas Convention	2.0(1.3)	1.9(1.3)	2.7(1.3)	2.3(1.3)	2.2(1.3)	2.9(.8)	1.4(.8)	2.0(1.4)	2.1(1.4)
040 1958 Fisheries Convention	1.8(1.2)	1.7(1.1)	2.3(1.4)	2.2(1.3)	2.1(1.3)	1.3(1.0)	1.3(.5)	1.7(1.3)	1.9(1.2)
041 IMCO Oil Pollution Conventions	1.5(.7)	1.2(.4)	2.0(.8)	2.1(.8)	1.2(.4)	1.4(.7)	1.6(.5)	1.2(.6)	1.1(.4)
042 Territorial sea width claimed	38(72)	22(45)	5(4)	5(4)	64(89)	7(6)	10(4)	30(52)	21(57)
043 Fisheries zone claimed	41(71)	44(68)	16(38)	16(36)	96(98)	9(6)	17(18)	36(57)	34(70)
044 Economic zone position	3.5(1.6)	3.5(1.4)	2.1(1.3)	2.5(1.5)	4.7(1.1)	2.3(1.4)	2.9(1.1)	3.0(1.4)	2.9(1.4)
045 Proven offshore oil per GNP	.055(.283)	.056(.256)	.011(.039)	.003(.014)	.008(.038)	.0001(.0004)	.305(.607)	.018(.067)	.001(.004)
046 Research vessels per GNP (1/1,000,000)	96(410)	120(717)	366(1,283)	294(1,210)	121(588)	83(98)	345(1,296)	.31(1.6)	88(?227)
047 Research vessels per shore length (1/10,000)	11(46)	2(5)	32(63)	24(57)	1(3)	23(26)	18(68)	1.0(3.7)	7.3(28)
048 Research vessels per no. scientists (10,000)	41(277)	10(52)	128(599)	114(577)	83(408)	.7(.8)	26(93)	1.4(7.2)	12.1(31)
049 Research vessels per naval vessels (1/1,000)	33(154)	98(373)	120(212)	105(209)	51(223)	28(26)	130(499)	20(63)	83(241)
050 Large naval vessels per coastal naval vessels	.22(.36)	.24(.39)	.76(1.1)	.78(1.1)	.38(.46)	.41(.59)	.047(.086)	.062(.217)	.234(.333)
051 Naval vessels per GNP (1/10,000)	80(108)	34(58)	28(29)	32(38)	37(35)	73(143)	72(71)	35(86)	74(104)

Marine Outputs	Low Political Competition (n = 52)	Med. Political Competition (n = 64)	High Political Competition (n = 26)	W. Europe & English Speaking (n = 29)	Latin America (n = 24)	USSR & Eastern Europe (n = 9)	Middle East & N. Africa (n = 19)	Sub-Saharan Africa (n = 34)	Southeast Asia (n = 27)
052 Naval vessels per population (1/10,000)	26(36)	13(24)	67(73)	62(70)	20(17)	52(66)	33(41)	5(8)	15(21)
053 Coastal naval vessels per 200-mile zone (1/10,000)	33(144)	1(3)	46(164)	9(24)	1(1)	49(61)	57(216)	3(1)	36(159)
054 Shipping flag tonnage per GNP (100)	3(13.6)	24.2(176)	1.7(3.6)	3.2(7.9)	3.0(13.5)	.4(.4)	74(323)	2.3(12.7)	3.4(11.7)
055 Shipping flag tonnage per seaborne trade	131(521)	217(909)	53(85)	142(287)	88(338)	55(37)	110(456)	157(681)	290(1,257)
056 Shipbuilding per GNP	2.0(7.0)	.2(.8)	11.8(20.3)	10.0(18.1)	.2(.6)	7.7(13.4)	.1(.4)	.01(.04)	2.1(9.9)
057 Seaborne trade per GNP	5.3(13.4)	9.3(18.8)	5.0(8.3)	2.5(3.8)	5.0(8.4)	.9(.9)	28.3(27.2)	3.7(8.1)	5.2(15.3)
058 Fish catch per GNP (1/100)	87(233)	33(72)	69(259)	64(246)	78(312)	7(7)	63(169)	39(55)	78(101)
059 Fish catch per potential (1/1,000,000)	87(147)	91(414)	125(201)	69(114)	21(56)	218(225)	68(183)	164(539)	93(175)
060 Fish imports per GNP	1.2(1.9)	2.3(5.0)	2.3(2.4)	1.6(1.2)	2.7(6.1)	1.0(1.1)	.9(2.0)	2.2(3.7)	2.0(4.4)
061 Fish exports per GNP	2.5(7.3)	4.7(22.3)	10.8(42.3)	9.4(40.2)	4.8(10.2)	.2(.2)	1.8(4.3)	1.9(6.2)	8.1(33.7)
062 Offshore oil prod. per GNP (1/100,000)	54(328)	73(410)	6(21)	2(8)	5(20)	0(0)	325(875)	32(142)	4(16)
063 UN LOS delegation size per GNP (1/10,000)	51(79)	146(308)	52(105)	56(121)	51(70)	7(8)	94(123)	131(182)	153(425)

defined according to processing characteristics. The first three columns are defined by degree of political competition. The next six correspond to various geographic regions in the world. For each cell in the table, two values are given, the average value followed by the standard deviation in parentheses. The standard deviation is a measure of consistency within the group—a small standard deviation means high consistency and little variety in the scores. High standard deviations means that the scores range markedly from one state to the next. In examining this table it is essential that values be interpreted comparatively because, in many instances, units are difficult to interpret otherwise. Some of the more subtle patterns will emerge later when factor analysis is employed, so the discussion here is limited to the most conspicuous differences among the nine groups.

The first seven rows (variables) in the table deal with the maritime and naval posture of the states. The group labeled USSR and Eastern Europe is dominant here. This is not surprising, since the Soviet Union is a leader in all categories and comprises 1/9 of this group—thus the average values are increased substantially. The West European group (which includes the U.S.A.) scores substantially lower since it contains a much larger number of countries (twenty-nine)—hence the influence of the United States is diluted. In the three variables dealing with shipping and seaborne trade, two groups are dominant, the High Political Competition and the Western European group. Again this is not surprising since these groups contain most of the dominant economic powers in the world, many of which are heavily dependent on foreign trade for their economic prosperity. It is worth mentioning that the High Political Competition and Western European groups overlap considerably.

The three variables pertaining directly to fisheries also tend to be dominated by the High Political Competition and Western European groups, although certain other groups have high scores on one of the three fisheries variables. But dominance in fishing catch, importing, and exporting seems to rest with those states with high political competition and/or those falling in the Western European group. Of course this should not lead to the inferential leap that political competition produces fishing dominance. Many of the major fishing states do have competitive political systems, for example, Japan, the United Kingdom, Iceland, and the United States, enough that the average for the group exceeds the rest of the world. There are, of course, leading fishing powers dispersed among the other groups, including the Soviet Union, Peru, Poland, and the German Democratic Republic.

Next is a group of five variables that deals with participation in certain marine-related international activities. Although the nature of the international cooperation represented in each is very different, the same trend seems to manifest itself in the dominance of the High Political Competition and Western European groups. But in most instances the differences among the nine groups are rather small. In many areas tabulated, the Soviet and Eastern European group is not far behind indicating interest and participation on their part.

Approximately in the middle of the table is a set of five variables indicating the degree of commitment to the four 1958 Geneva Conventions as well as the IMCO Oil Pollution Convention and Amendments. The scale used here is a delicate one. Average scores of 2.0 and above indicate at least some degree of commitment to the conventions; thus the same two groups, the Western European and High Political Competition, have a degree of commitment significantly higher than any other group. Some other groups cross the 2.0 threshold on certain of the five conventions, but not on all. For example, the Soviet group scores relatively highly on the Territorial Seas, High Seas, and Continental Shelf Conventions. The greatest difference between the High Political Competition and Western European groups is on the IMCO Pollution Conventions. This may be attributable to the fact that many smaller states do not engage in significant numbers of activities covered by the convention.

The next three variables pertain to types of offshore zones claimed, or, in the case of the exclusive economic zone, to the preference indicated in U.N. Law of the Sea Conference debates. Here, more than in any of the other variables, one clearly sees the split between the developing and developed states with much narrower and more limited claims being asserted by the latter group. Not unexpectedly, Latin America leads the rest of the world in width of claimed territorial sea and fisheries zone. Latin America also has taken by far the most comprehensive position on the amount of coastal state control within economic zones.

The balance of the variables are derivatives or combinations of the previously discussed ones. As such many of them give a clearer idea of the importance of certain marine activities in comparison to the overall size of a state. The first thing one notices is that the dominance of the Middle East in all petroleum categories continues even in the relative variables, for example, their Offshore Oil Production per GNP.

The last variable, UN LOS Delegation Size per GNP gives an indication of states' level of interest in the future law of the sea treaty, considering that the smaller countries simply cannot afford the huge delegations that are sent by the larger states. Interestingly, when the normalizing effect of GNP level is introduced, the developing countries, specifically Sub-Saharan Africa and Southeast Asia, have the most commitment.

In general, it does not seem that the elements of processing identified in the model have too significant an effect on the marine-policy ouputs. Obviously, the rich countries, whether or not they are politically competitive score higher on indices of economic development, marine or otherwise. The political competition attribute itself seems to have been an unimportant determinant of marine policy, at least when taking the level of economic development into account. Region of the world seems to have some, albeit a minimum, effect on the policy outputs. The preponderance of the developed countries again comes through here since they are concentrated in two of the six regions. One also finds the expected oil dominance in the Middle East and the most ambitious current and potential claims to hydrospace in Latin America. On balance it would seem that the few elements of the processing section identified here are not of paramount importance in marine policy making. It is expected that more comprehensive techniques employed later may uncover more subtle influences between the processing and the policy outputs.

Several things should be clear from table 3-2. The first is that it can become very difficult to sift through hundreds of countries and scores of variables to see what overall trends and patterns exist. The problem is magnified when one considers that this table contains less than 400 pieces of information whereas the entire data set contains over 12,000. Thus, it is evident that some method of handling the mass of information while still extracting the meaning is essential. This can be accomplished by factor analysis, which is the approach taken next.

Factor-Analysis Techniques

Firestone has claimed that factor analysis can be used to bring a quantitative systems approach to bear on the problem of political-systems analysis.[2] Systems analysis, many aspects of which are employed here, deals with a number of inter-related elements—supposedly any change in one element will affect all the others. Factor analysis also begins with relationships among elements or variables. *Factor analysis* is a technique or procedure "by which regularity and order in phenomena can be discerned."[3] The principal difference between systems analysis and factor analysis is that the latter demands that all relationships be expressed in concrete, mathematical terms like the correlation coefficients discussed earlier. All factor analysis begins with a data matrix consisting of cases (countries in this instance) each of which has a score of value on each of a number of variables. The first computations step is calculating correlations among each possible pair of variables. When the number of variables is small, correlational results are sufficient, since simple inspection will reveal all significant interrelationships. However, when the number of variables is large, a way of looking for order and simplicity of expression is needed. This is where factor analysis is useful—it assumes that the "correlation matrix contains or is permeated by a complex configuration of shared variance that can be expressed in terms of a limited number of common factors."[4]

If the factor analysis is properly performed, the results may be a factor solution yielding factors containing almost all the original information but with much greater parsimony and economy of description.[5] Factor analysis creates a new correlation matrix with relationships between all variables and the newly created entities, the factors. Theoretically, the number of factors can be as large as the number of variables, in which case no economy of expression results, but in most instances the correlations between variables and factors become low after a small number of factors has been constructed. Hence, most factors can usually be eliminated leaving a smaller number, typically 10 percent of the number of variables, that explain most of the pattern in the original variables.

Interpreting factor matrices is done by grouping those variables that load (correlate) highly with each factor. Correlations with the factors must be squared to obtain the amount of variance in a given variable accounted for by the factor. Thus far it has been assumed that the factors themselves are uncorrelated—this is not always the case, as will be discussed when the problem of rotation is examined.

Recalling the set of input, processing, and output variables, it should be obvious that the goal of factor analysis here is to reduce the number of variables to a smaller number of synthetic or conceptual variables called factors. This process can work in two ways. First, the data can be arranged with countries defining the rows in a data matrix and variables corresponding to the columns. Factor analyzing a matrix like this will produce (hopefully) a discrete number of factors that are highly correlated with the variables. In other words, a large number of variables have been collapsed into a much smaller number of factors, with those variables having similar characteristics being grouped with the same factor. If the data matrix is reversed, so the variables define the rows, factor analysis produces factors that tend to collapse countries into groups or blocs that have similar characteristics. Although the computational procedures are nearly identical, there are subtle differences between handling the original data matrix and its reverse. These distinctions, although beyond the scope of this presentation, are discussed elsewhere.[6] There are names for these two different types of factor analyses. When the variables are collapsed into a smaller number of factors, it is termed R analysis. When the cases or countries defining the columns are collapsed into groups having similar behavior, it is called Q analysis.

An important, and somewhat involved aspect of factor analysis is rotation. The following example, adapted from Rummel's work, may help to clarify rotation.[7] Assume that two factors account for most of the pattern or variation in seven variables—the situation may be represented graphically.

The seven numbered lines in figure 3-1 correspond to seven variables, each of which can be plotted relative to two factors. The variables cluster together into two distinct groups. This suggests that factor analysis will work, that is, the pattern in the original variables can be simplified into a smaller group of synthetic variables or factors. Rotation is used to move the factors so they correspond more closely to the positions of the different variables. Rotation relates to the way in which the factors are moved. In figure 3-1, if the factors were rotated orthogonally, they would move as a single structure. Factors 1 and 2 would remain uncorrelated with each other, that is, there would continue to be a 90° angle between them. In the example, a 45° clockwise rotation would place the factors much closer to the two clusters of variables. However, it can be seen that rotating the first factor 35° and the second factor 60° would place

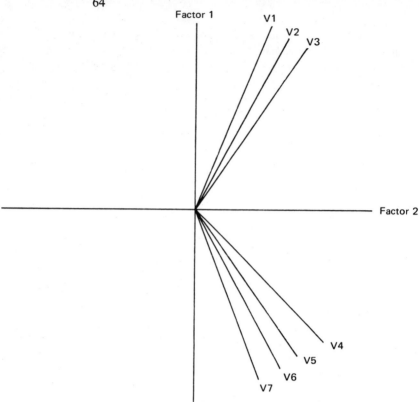

Figure 3-1. Explanation of Factor Rotation

them in the best possible positions to identify the pattern present in the original variables. In this case oblique rotation would have to be employed—it has the advantage of fitting the variable more precisely. It has the disadvantage of introducing a complicating influence, the fact that the factors themselves can be intercorrelated. Orthogonal rotation is neater and easier to interpret, whereas oblique rotation is likely to produce a better fit with the data and is more realistic. The feeling seems to be that in most instances little is gained by using the oblique technique. In the few cases where the oblique rotation has been employed, correlations among factors have been low, suggesting that orthogonal rotation would have been equally appropriate.[8]

On balance, it can be stated that factor analysis is a powerful technique with exceptional data-reduction capabilities. It seems that such a procedure is appropriate to the marine-policy model employed here. There are problems and limitations with the technique. For example, it assumes that relationships between variables are linear, which may ignore many strong nonlinear associations. Nevertheless at this formative, model- and theory-building stage, factor analysis seems to be suited to the task.

R-Factor Analysis of Complete Data Matrix

Table 3-3 provides the results of an orthogonally rotated *R*-factor analysis of all the variables. The oblique technique of rotation was also tested, but the inter-factor correlations were low enough so orthogonal rotation was thought to be adequate. Even a casual examination of the table reveals a major strength and one of the major weaknesses of the technique. On the positive side, factor analysis has indeed been able to reduce the number of variables to a much smaller number of factors. In fact, the ten factors together account for about 65 percent of the total variation, a respectable figure considering the diversity of the original variables. On the negative side, it can be somewhat difficult to tell exactly what the different factors mean, since each must be identified on the basis of the variables with which it correlates (loads) highly. To eliminate the interference of less significant variables, only those loadings stronger than .35 have been included in the table.

Factor A has identified a set of characteristics that include inputs and out-puts, both marine and nonmarine. This factor might be termed Global Size-Power since it loads most highly with things like land area, GNP, science manpower, and number of vessels of all kinds. It is also clear that a major component of this factor involves the capacity to have a truly global presence. This can be seen in the very high loadings with long-range vessels as well as in the lower, but still significant, loadings with bilateral treaties, fisheries commission membership and seaborne trade. This Global Size-Power factor consists of a set of behaviors comprised of power, largess, and the inclination and capacity to use the power in a global context.

Factor B identifies a group of characteristics containing all the significant loadings with the processing variables. The variables that play important roles in this factor also show a high living standard manifested in GNP, GNP per capita, and literacy rate. Variation identified in this pattern also relates to internationalism, in the sense of relinquishing some degree of sovereignty to international organizations. Note the high loadings with international organiza-tion membership, multilateral treaty making, and all the variables concerned with the support and use of the International Court of Justice. Therefore, this factor might be called Prosperity and Competition-International Cooperation. Interestingly, none of the input variables loads highly with this factor suggesting that no definite set of characteristics predisposes the type of behavior aggregated by this factor.

Factor C is extremely easy to label. Unmistakingly it has identified marine dependence, that is, the tendency for certain states to have large maritime boundaries, zones, and so on in proportion to their land masses. Interestingly, these same states also tend to have the largest delegations to the Third United Nations Law of the Sea Conference, at least in proportion to their economic size. The factor is called Relative Coast Importance.

Table 3–3

Orthogonally Rotated Factor Matrix for All Variables

	Factor A	Factor B	Factor C	Factor D	Factor E	Factor F	Factor G	Factor H	Factor I	Factor J
Nonmarine										
I1 Land area	.81									
I2 Arable land					.45					
I3 Oil reserves (ultimate onshore)				-.40				-.48		
I4 Oil reserves (proven onshore)	.57			.67						
I5 Arable land per land area	.84									
Marine Inputs										
I6 Seabed area (200 meters)					.89					
I7 Seabed area (3,000 meters)					.86					
I8 Seabed area (200 miles)	.36			.74						
I9 Shoreline length					.88					
I10 Oil reserves (ultimate offshore)				-.38				-.46		
I11 Oil reserves (proven offshore)				.87						
I12 Semienclosed seas bordered	.41				.49					
I13 International straits bordered					.57			.37		
I14 Fish potential within 200 miles (%)									-.37	
I15 Seabed 200 meters per land area			.88						-.35	
I16 Seabed 300 meters per land area			.73							
I17 Seabed 200 miles per land area			.90							
I18 Seabed 3,000 meters per seabed 200 meters										
I19 Seabed 200 miles per seabed 200 meters										
I20 Shoreline length per land area			.72							
I21 Oil off ultimate per oil on ultimate										
I22 High fish poten. per seabed 200 miles					.80					
Processing										
P1 Degree political competition		.51								
P3 Years of independence		.50								
P4 Age of constitution		.60								
Nonmarine Outputs										
O1 Literacy rate		.47								
O2 Population	.47									

#	Variable	F1	F2	F3	F4	F5	F6	F7	F8	F9	F10	F11
03	Population growth rate		−.42		.44							
04	Gross national product	.62	.60									
05	Science manpower	.92										
06	Oil production onshore	.72			.51							
07	Bilateral treaties (number of)	.57	.73									
08	Multilateral treaties (number of)		.79	−.48								
09	International organ. (no. member of)										.47	
010	Dispute settlement treaties (no. of)		.81									
011	ICJ use treaties (number of)		.83									
012	ICJ support		.63									
013	Copper production	.64				.36						
014	Nickel production					.72						
015	Manganese production	.72										
016	Cobalt production									.39		
017	Population per area											
018	GNP per population		.66									
019	Scientists per population	.61	.52									

Marine Outputs

#	Variable	F1	F2	F3	F4	F5	F6	F7	F8	F9	F10	F11
020	Research vessels	.87										
021	Naval vessels (large)	.91										
022	Naval vessels (coastal)	.73										
023	Submarines	.94										
024	Merchant shipping tonnage		.46					.60	−.46			
025	Shipbuilding								−.77			
026	Seaborne trade		.66									
027	Fish catch	.44							−.64			
028	Fish imports		.78									
029	Fish exports		.39						−.59			
030	Oil production (offshore)					.78						
031	Seafood consumption per capita								−.43			
032	Fishery Commission membership	.37	.55						−.46			
033	UN LOS Conference delegation size	.45	.65			.43						
034	IOC membership						.39	.42				.36
035	SCOR membership		.73			.38		.57				
036	U.N. Seabed Committee											
037	'58 Territorial Sea Convention						.85					
038	'58 Continental Shelf Convention						.84					
039	'58 High Seas Convention						.81					
040	'58 Fisheries Convention						.82					
041	IMCO Oil Pollution Conventions		.53									

Table 3-3—*Continued*

	Factor A	Factor B	Factor C	Factor D	Factor E	Factor F	Factor G	Factor H	Factor I	Factor J
042 Territorial sea width								.70		
043 Fisheries zone width								.71		
044 Economic zone restrictiveness								.53		
045 Proven off oil per GNP				.88						
046 Research vessels per GNP							.92			
047 Research vessels per shoreline length										.68
048 Research vessels per no. scientists							.63			
049 Research vessels per naval vessels							.91			
050 Large naval vessels per coastal naval vessels		.48								
051 Naval vessels per GNP					.63					
052 Naval vessels per population										.36
053 Coastal naval vessels per 200-mile zone area										.70
054 Shipping flag tonnage per GNP							.81			
055 Shipping flag tonnage per seaborne trade										
056 Shipbuilding per GNP		.39							-.65	
057 Seaborne trade per GNP			.36	.48			.35			
058 Fish catch per GNP										
059 Fish catch per fish potential w/i 200 miles										.42
060 Fish imports per GNP										
061 Fish exports per GNP										
062 Offshore oil prod. per GNP					.73					
063 UN LOS delegation per GNP			.80							

Note: Contains all correlations (loadings) greater than .35 or less than −.35.

Factor D isolates most of the variables relating to petroleum. Two of the loadings (ultimate onshore oil reserves and ultimate offshore oil reserves) are negative; this is due to the type of scale adopted for the variables—it does not indicate an inverse relationship. The highest loadings are proven offshore oil reserves and offshore oil production as a portion of GNP. However, since onshore oil is also involved in the pattern it is labeled Oil Resources.

The strongest relationships in factor E bear on the coastal situation of states. Especially high loadings are shoreline length and continental-shelf area. Also important is the percentage of the economic zone having high fisheries potential (variable I22). Certain of the other significant loadings, specifically semienclosed seas bordered and straits bordered, probably can be subsumed under the other relationships. For example, if a state has a long coastline, one would expect (on the average) it to border more international straits. This factor can appropriately be called Coastal Size.

Factor F is the most straightforward of all the patterns. It loads highly only with the four Geneva Conventions and with IOC membership. However, since the relationships with the four conventions are the strongest, it can appropriately be called Acceptance of 1958 Conventions.

Factor G contains relatively few loadings achieving the .35 criterion. But significant relationships do exist with research vessels relative to the overall size of states as well as with seaborne trade and shipping tonnage in both relative and absolute terms. This factor is somewhat more difficult to label but it might be called Marine Science-Merchant Shipping Importance. Factor H contains a variety of loadings, which when taken together might be called Exclusive Claims Oil-Fish Potential.

The last two factors, I and J, are extremely difficult to label. Although some significant relationships remain, the overall magnitudes are lower than in the previous instances. This is expected, since most of the important regularity and pattern has been accounted for in the first eight factors.

Table 3-4 is a factor matrix very similar to that presented in table 3-3, with the important difference that table 3-4 contains only the marine variables. To avoid confusion the factors in this second table have been numbered rather than lettered.

Factor 1 in table 3-4 relates to a wide range of marine variables, so wide a range, in fact, that a simple label is illusive. But so many different variables load highly with the factor that it is important. Three loadings are greater than 0.80, but these three are somewhat diverse, fish imports, UN Law of the Sea Conference delegation size, and number of representatives in SCOR. For purposes of easy identification, a goal of this exercise, it may be best to omit factor 1. This points out one of the shortcomings of factor analysis, that it, it is a mathematical technique that may produce results difficult to describe in common-sense terms.

Table 3-4
Orthogonally Rotated Factor Matrix for Marine Variables

	Factor 1	Factor 2	Factor 3	Factor 4	Factor 5	Factor 6	Factor 7	Factor 8	Factor 9	Factor 10
Marine Inputs										
I6 Seabed area (200 meters)			-.65							
I7 Seabed area (3,000 meters)			-.72							
I8 Seabed area (200 miles)			-.64							
I9 Shoreline length			-.63							
I10 Oil reserves (ultimate offshore)										
I11 Oil reserves (proven offshore)										
I12 Semienclosed seas bordered										
I13 International straits bordered									.58	
I14 Fish potential within 200 miles (%)			-.51							
I15 Seabed 200 meters per land area		.93								
I16 Seabed 3,000 meters per land area		.76								
I17 Seabed 200 miles per land area		.90								
I18 Seabed 3,000 meters per seabed 200 meters										
I19 Seabed 200 miles per seabed 200 meters										
I20 Shoreline length per land area		.62								
I21 Oil off ultimate per oil on ultimate								.36		
I22 High fish poten. per seabed 200 miles	-.64									.53
Marine Outputs										
O20 Research vessels	-.54								.78	
O21 Naval vessels (large)	-.48								.83	
O22 Naval vessels (coastal)									.77	
O23 Submarines									.91	
O24 Merchant shipping tonnage	-.40				-.62		-.48			
O25 Shipbuilding							-.73			
O26 Seaborne trade	-.74									
O27 Fish catch							-.67		.42	
O28 Fish imports	-.81									
O29 Fish exports	-.41						-.75			
O30 Oil production (offshore)	-.38					.71				
O31 Seafood consumption per capita							-.50			
O32 Fishery Commission membership	-.71						-.45			

	I	II	III	IV	V	VI	VII
033 UN LOS Conference delegation size	−.82						.35
034 IOC membership		−.36	.42				
035 SCOR membership	.81						
036 U.N. Seabed Committee							
037 '58 Territorial Sea Convention			.89				
038 '58 Continental Shelf Convention			.85				
039 '58 High Seas Convention			.87				
040 '58 Fisheries Convention			.86				
041 IMCO Oil Pollution Conventions	−.51						.37
042 Territorial sea width		−.48					
043 Fisheries zone width		−.52					
044 Economic zone restrictiveness		−.61					
045 Proven off oil per GNP					.88		
046 Research vessels per GNP				−.91			
047 Research vessels per shoreline length						.85	
048 Research vessels per no. scientists				−.62			
049 Research vessels per naval vessels				−.91			
050 Large naval vessels per coastal naval vessels	−.74						
051 Naval vessels per GNP		−.42					
052 Naval vessels per population							
053 Coastal naval vessels per 200-mile zone area				−.83		.85	
054 Shipping flag tonnage per GNP							.68
055 Shipping flag tonnage per seaborne trade				−.73			
056 Shipbuilding per GNP							
057 Seaborne trade per GNP	.42				.54		
058 Fish catch per GNP				−.38		.60	.62
059 Fish catch per fish potential w/i 200 miles							
060 Fish imports per GNP							
061 Fish exports per GNP							
062 Offshore oil prod. per GNP					.82		
063 U.N. LOS delegation per GNP	.83						.88

Note: Contains all correlations (loadings) greater than .35 or less than −.35.

In sharp contrast, factor 2 loads highly with four variables; the four are also interrelated. This factor corresponds very closely with factor C in table 3-3 suggesting that this pattern is retained even when the nonmarine variables are omitted. The most appropriate title for the factor is Relative Coastal Marine Size. The relativity is very important, since another factor has identified absolute coastal size.

Factor 3 neatly isolates two distinct sets of characteristics. The first set relates to the absolute size of the coastal area. Included here are seabed areas and shoreline length. The second set of variables deals with the size and nature of zonal claims by coastal states. All three relevant variables load at high levels. This factor can be labeled Zone Size and Claim. This factor has no good parallel in the factors identified in table 3-3.

Factor 4 relates very strongly with the four 1958 Geneva Conventions. In fact these are the only high loadings. This pattern bears very close resemblance to factor F in table 3-3. As before, the factor will be called Geneva Conventions' Acceptance.

Factor 5 relates most strongly to the relative importance of marine scientific research and to the relative and absolute importance of merchant shipping. It corresponds very closely to factor G discussed earlier. It is called Relative Marine Scientific Research Importance-Merchant Shipping.

Factor 6 loads very strongly with *all* the offshore oil variables. The only other variable involved to a significant degree is Seaborne Trade per GNP (loading .54). This is probably not important independently of the petroleum variables. One would expect that petroleum would account for a sizeable amount of the seaborne trade of the countries involved. This factor, which will be called Offshore Oil, corresponds fairly closely to factor D in table 3-3.

Factor 7 has no very high loadings—none is greater than .80. But it has highlighted a series of variables relating both to fisheries and merchant shipping importance; it can be appropriately labeled Shipping-Fishing Importance. Factor 8 has identified a number of important marine variables, but arriving at a simple description is difficult. Factor 9 is clearly similar to factor A in table 3-3. It is called Marine Size-Wealth. Loadings on factor 9 are not as high as those on factor A, suggesting that much national size and wealth is not dependent on marine characteristics, hardly a surprising fact. Factor 10 relates strongly to only three variables, Shipping Flag Tonnage per Seaborne Trade, Fish Catch per GNP, and Fish Exports per GNP. Arguably, then, the factor can be called Relative Flag Tonnage and Shipping Importance.

The implications of tables 3-3 and 3-4 are clear. It has been demonstrated that it is possible to reduce some 90 variables to a much smaller number of factors and still preserve much of the original meaning and pattern. More precisely, the factors account for about two thirds of the variance present in the original variables. This means that one of the goals of factor analysis has been achieved, that is, data reduction. From the factors presented in the two tables, one can discern general patterns of variable regularity. This is very important information not intuitively obvious and not easily obtainable in other ways. The most important aspects of the individual factors have already been discussed, but a few general observations can be offered. It is not surprising that one factor in both tables identifies size and wealth. This is quite similar to the results of many earlier factor-analysis works.[9] The rest of the factors seem to revolve about several major themes. The magnitude and kind of coastal activity is one such theme. Interestingly, two distinct patterns emerge, one relating to the absolute magnitude of coastal size and the other coastal size relative to overall national characteristics. This finding in and of itself casts doubt on numerous analyses of national marine policies, many of which fail to distinguish between marine activities per se and the value of such activities when compared with the totality of states' activities.

In both tables a single factor loaded highly with all the 1958 Geneva Conventions and with none of the other variables. This implies that states relationships to those four conventions are a unique set of behaviors not subsumable within any other pattern. For example, one might have thought that a pattern like that of factor C (Relative Coastal Importance) might have isolated the 1958 Geneva Convention variables on the theory that countries to whom the coast was important would have a consistent posture toward the 1958 Conventions. This was not the case; instead the 1958 Conventions all relate to another factor that is, by definition, unrelated to all the other factors. In both tables, a single factor has identified oil resources again suggesting a unique pattern. This is somewhat surprising since it would have been reasonable to assume that oil wealth bore some relationship to continental-shelf size or to land area.

Especially when all the variables were included, one factor very clearly identified magnitude of zonal claims. Again it should be emphasized that zonal claims might have fitted well with certain other patterns, but this did not occur. In the area of fishing and shipping importance there was the same, unmistakable tendency for the factor-analysis procedures to isolate the relative from the absolute importance of these activities.

Factor Scores of Countries

Although the factors themselves are very important and revealing, they provide little direct information about individual country characteristics. Such characteristics are enormously important since state behavior is the basic building block of marine policies. It is possible to use the factor-analysis results to explore individual country positions by computing factor scores. Factor scores are simply values given to each country on each computed factor. The magnitude of a factor score depends both on the factor loadings and on the country's scores on the variables. For example, looking at factor A, one would expect the United States to have a very high factor score because the United States has large land area, considerable science manpower, many large naval vessels, and so on. In short, since the United States has scores much above average on the variables that load highly with the factor, it will have a high factor score.

Factor scores are normalized so they have an average value of 0.0 and a standard deviation of 1.0. This means roughly speaking that two thirds of country factor scores can be expected to fall between -1.0 and +1.0. Any score lower than 0.0 is below average—any score greater greater than 0.0 is above average. Statistically, any factors greater than +1.0 or less than -1.0 are unusual and interesting for the purposes of this inquiry since such scores represent extremes. The figures that follow place countries on axes according to their factor scores on certain pairs of the factors. It was necessary to be quite selective in the choice of factors since several hundred possible graphs can be generated from the 20 factors in tables 3-3 and 3-4. To make the plots less cluttered, only those countries with somewhat extreme scores have been included. Extreme scores were defined as greater than .50 (or less than -.50) on both factors or greater than +.75 (or less than -.75) on either one of the factors. The only exceptions to this rule were the five countries whose marine policies were examined in chapter 2. These five have been included on each graph irrespective of the magnitude of their scores. In some cases when the factor scores were very large (for example, the USSR on the Global Size-Power factor), it was necessary to represent the scores as merely extremes rather than as the actual value—such adjustments should have no effect on interpreting the graphs. On all the graphs that follow, letter abbreviations are given instead of the unwieldy country names; a list of these abbreviations is contained in appendix A.

Most of the graphs follow the usual mathematical convention for large and small values, that is, top is largest and bottom smallest, right is greatest and left smallest. However, in a few instances the standard procedure has been reversed because of negative loadings in the factor-analysis results. In these cases "+" or "-" is indicated on the coordinate axes to alert the reader. In figures 3-2 to 3-10, certain groups of states have been circled; these are the blocs that seem especially significant. Most of the graphs use factor scores derived from the analysis of only the marine variables. It was thought that this provided the most straightforward approach and minimized the chance of confusing the effect of marine and nonmarine attributes. It should be borne in mind that one would not expect to find linear relationships in any of the graphs, because factor analysis of the variety employed here identifies factors uncorrelated with one another. Thus the reason for plotting factor scores is to identify clusters of countries that have similar values on both of the factors.

Figure 3-2 compares factor scores on factor 3 (Zone Size and Claim) and Factor 4 (Geneva Convention Acceptance). Four groups of countries seem to stand out here—each has been circled on the figure. In the upper left quadrant one finds a group of poor landlocked states—as one might expect them to have

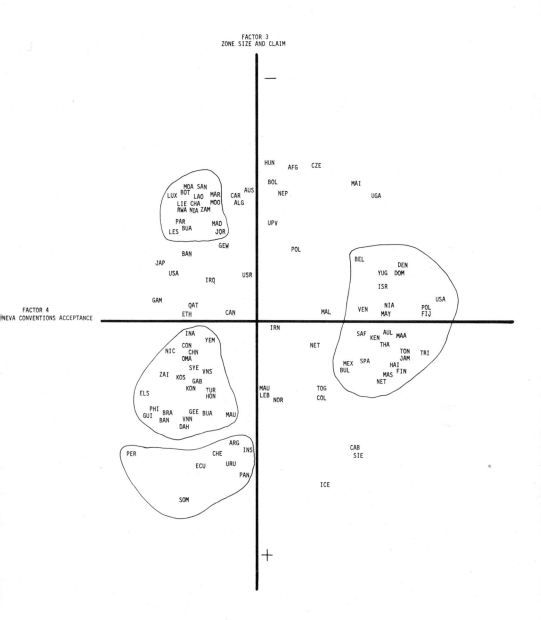

Figure 3–2. Relationship between Zone Size and Claim and Geneva Conventions'
Acceptance

small marine zones and usually assert no claim to maritime territory. Additionally, they have tended to avoid four 1958 Geneva Conventions. By contrast, those states in the upper right section of the graph are also landlocked, but most do have some involvement with the 1958 Conventions. Most of this group of landlocked states are more highly developed, for example, Hungary and Czechoslovakia. In the lower left quadrant, one finds two distinct groups of countries. The larger and more moderate group (the one closer to the origin) contains a number of Third World nations all with above average Zone Size-Claim and below average acceptance of the 1958 Conventions. It is a diverse group containing Brazil and China along with many small states. In this same quadrant is a group of states having much more extensive zone claims and zone sizes. Included here are Chile, Ecuador, and Peru, charter members of the 200-mile club. With the exception of Somalia and Indonesia, all of the states are Latin American. One of the more interesting things about these three groups is that there is almost an identical (low) acceptance of the four 1958 Conventions. One might have anticipated that the degree of acceptance would bear some relationship to the type and size of marine zone claimed.

On the right side of the graph is a group of countries having a wide degree of acceptance of the 1958 Conventions—each is at least one standard deviation above the mean. The group contains the United States along with Third World, East European, and Latin American countries. The lesson seems to be that acceptance of the 1958 Conventions has little to do with political ideology or the size of the marine zone adjacent to a state.

Figure 3–3 compares factor 3 (Zone Size-Claim) with factor 9 (Marine Size-Wealth). Four country groupings seem significant here. In the upper left one finds a group of landlocked and geographically disadvantaged states who possess low levels of marine size and wealth and, not unexpectedly, small marine zones and claims to such zones. In the lower left quadrant is a group consisting mostly of Latin American states with much greater-than-average zone size and zonal claims, but still with below average Marine Size-Wealth. The large number of countries in this group suggests that the extent of coastal-state claims advanced by states may have little bearing on the actual wealth potential in coastal waters. In the lower right quadrant is a small group of states drawn from various regions having the combination of above average marine size-wealth and above-average zonal claims. At least in statistical terms, this would seem like a rational position for states to take. At the extreme right of the graph one finds the United States, the USSR, and China. Expectedly, these three states rate very highly on Marine Size-Wealth. There are differences in the Zone Size-Claim of the three with the USSR having the most modest claim, the United States about average for the world, and China having an above average zone size and zone claim.

Figure 3–4 relates factor 2 (Relative Coastal Marine Size) to factor 4 (Acceptance of the 1958 Geneva Conventions). Only two significant groupings

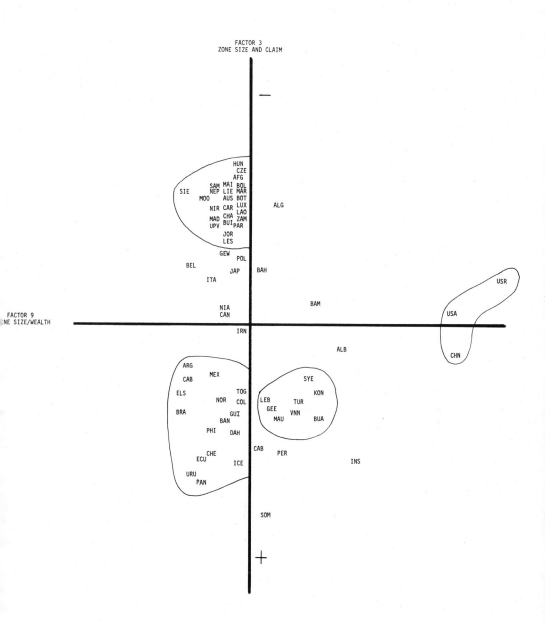

Figure 3-3. Relationship between Zone Size and Claim and Marine Size and Wealth

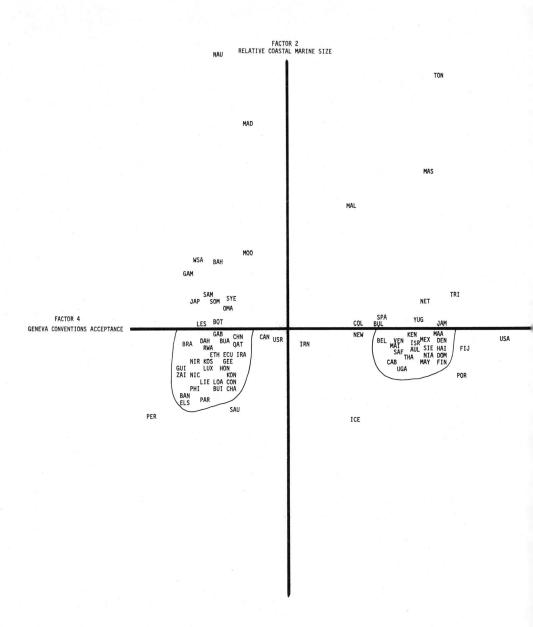

Figure 3-4. Relationship between Relative Coastal Marine Size and Geneva Conventions' Acceptance

appear. One, in the lower left quadrant, contains a group of countries having a low level of association with the 1958 Conventions and slightly lower than average relative coastal marine size. This bloc contains many Latin American and African states and a smattering of states from other regions—it includes both landlocked and large coastal states. The reason for this apparent inconsistency is, of course, that some states may have large coasts in absolute terms, but their coastal marine size in comparison to the totality of their activities may still be small—it is these states that form part of this group. In the lower right quadrant one finds a group of states having almost exactly the same level of comparative marine importance, but significantly greater association with the 1958 Conventions. This bloc contains members from Latin America (Mexico and Venezuela) as well as European and African states. The only particular pattern seems to be that most of the Latin American states were contained in the group that has avoided the 1958 Conventions.

In the upper portion of the graph, one finds only five states with very high scores on the Relative Coastal Marine Size factor: Malta, Mauritius, the Maldive Islands, Nauru, and Tonga. All of them, of course, are islands and small islands at that. Interestingly, even though these five have the greatest levels of coastal marine size, they exhibit no consistent pattern in their relationship with the 1958 Conventions, which is further evidence of the irregular way in which countries have ratified or refused to ratify the conventions.

Figure 3–5 compares factor 3 (Zone Size-Claim) with factor 2 (Relative Coastal Marine Size). Three different groupings stand out here. First, in the lower left quadrant, is a group with much greater than average zonal size and zonal claims and with slightly below average values on factor 3. The states encompassed here are a varied group including Latin American states as well as the German Democratic Republic and Cambodia. Perhaps surprising is the inclusion of Peru and Iceland in this group, both of which are leading coastal fishing states. Referring to table 3–4 explains this—the highly loading variables do not relate specifically to fishing but to magnitudes of coastal regions. Thus, one would expect the fishing dependence of these two states to be accommodated in those factors bearing more directly on fisheries.

In the lower right quadrant is a group of states including West European states, at the extreme as well as many of the world's landlocked states. These states all have below-average coastal marine importance as well as much below-average claims to coastal resources. In the upper right quadrant is a bloc of six states having lower-than-average zone size and zone claims, but above average coastal marine importance. These nations in spite of the importance of their coastal regions have for various reasons generally not asserted wide zonal claims.

Figure 3–6 again considers factor 3 (Zone Size-Claim), but this time compares it with factor 6 (Offshore Oil). As might be expected, relatively few states have high scores on the Offshore Oil factor. Saudia Arabia, Kuwait, and Qatar form a group of three at the extreme right of the graph. Another group

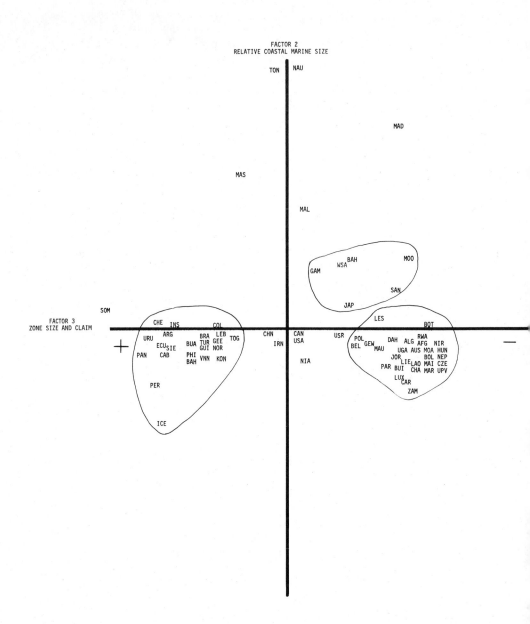

Figure 3–5. Relationship between Relative Coastal Marine Size and Zone Size and Claim

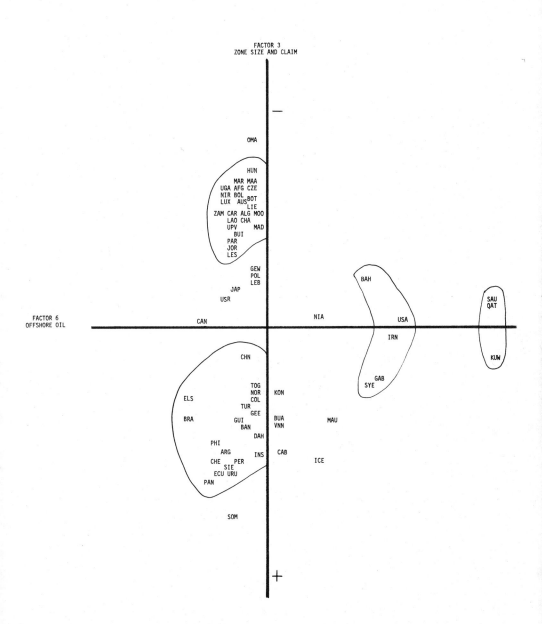

Figure 3-6. Relationship between Zone Size and Claim and Offshore Oil

in the middle right of the graph includes the Bahamas, the United States, Iran, and Southern Yemen states with high offshore oil potential—interestingly, both of these groups straddle the origin suggesting there is no relationship between offshore oil and zonal size and claim. On the left side of the graph are two other groupings, the top one containing landlocked and geographically disadvantaged states all of which have below average scores on both factors; in the lower left quadrant is a group consisting mostly of Third World countries, many of which have extensive marine zones and claims to these zones. Included here are most Latin American states along with a few anomalies like East Germany.

Figure 3–7 compares factor 4 (Acceptance of 1958 Geneva Conventions) with factor 7 (Shipping-Fishing Importance). In the extreme left portion of the graph one finds many of the world's major fishing powers: Peru, Japan, Norway, Iceland, and Denmark. Note that they are spread out along the vertical dimension suggesting little consistency among them in their relation to the 1958 Conventions. Peru and Japan, respectively, the foremost coastal and distant-water fishing states, have both avoided the 1958 Conventions. Three other groupings are in evidence. In the upper left quadrant are seven states drawn from several regions, each of which has wide acceptance of the 1958 Conventions *and* above-average fishing and shipping importance. In the lower half of the graph one finds two groups. Both groups have tended to avoid the 1958 Conventions and differ principally in the degree of fishing and shipping importance. There is little pattern to the difference between these groups except that fewer Latin countries are contained in the left group, that is, the group possessing above average shipping and fishing importance.

Figure 3–8 describes the relationship between Relative Flag Tonnage and Shipping Importance and Acceptance of the 1958 Geneva Conventions. Most evident here is that no group of states scores highly on both characteristics. One finds three rather distinct groupings defined mainly according to posture vis-à-vis the conventions. At the extreme right are Iceland, the Maldive Islands, and Peru. In the lower left quadrant is a diverse group of Third World countries all of which have slightly below average Relative Fishing and Shipping Importance and much below average degree of Acceptance of the 1958 Geneva Conventions.

Figure 3–9 differs from all preceding plots in that fewer states are represented. This, of course, means that the states of the world showed less variation in their scores with a greater number failing to make the cutoff points. However, four clusters are in evidence. The first in the lower half of the graph contains states with about average coastal size, but much below average both in prosperity and in internal political competition. Towards the top of the graph one finds the Western Democracies, which possess high living standards, domestic political competition, but who vary widely in their degree of coastal size. Towards the middle one finds two small groups with above average levels of prosperity and political competition, but different levels of coastal size.

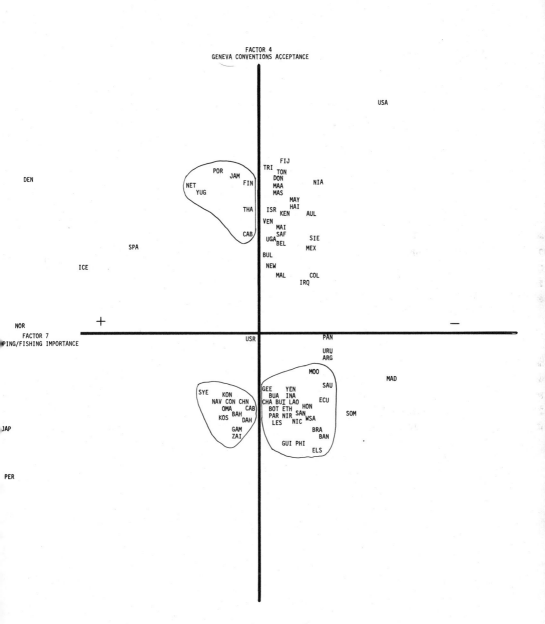

Figure 3-7. Relationship between Geneva Conventions' Acceptance and Shipping-Fishing Importance

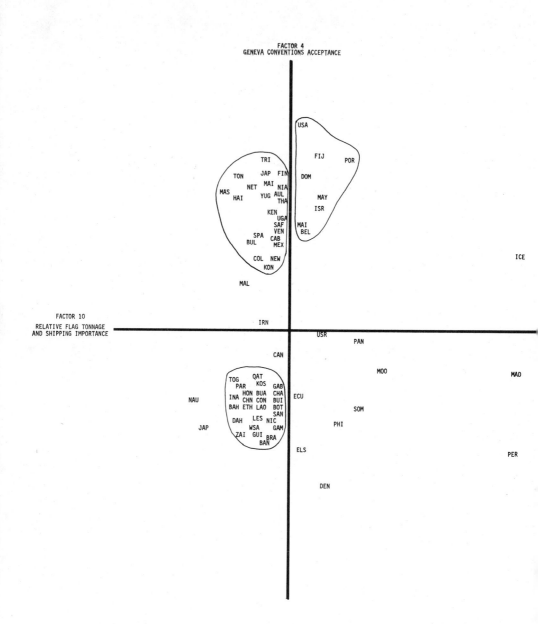

Figure 3-8. Relationship between Geneva Conventions' Acceptance and Relative Flag Tonnage and Shipping Importance

85

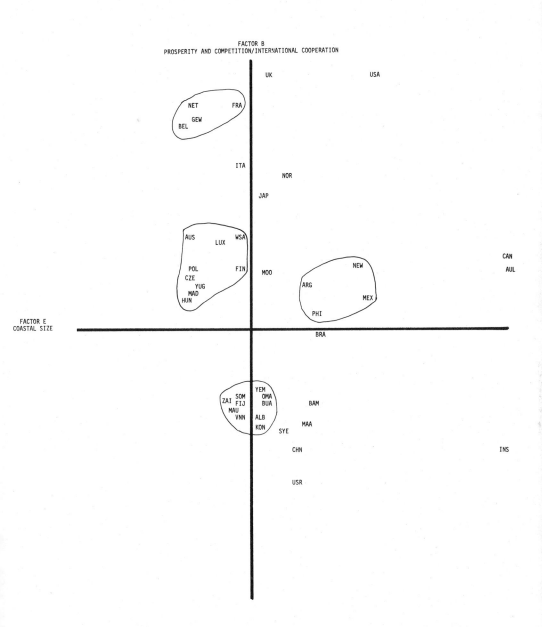

Figure 3-9. Relationship between Prosperity and Competition-International Cooperation and Coastal Size

Figure 3-10 compares factor A (Size-Wealth) with factor H (Exclusive Claims and Oil-Fish Potential). The two circled groups differ principally according to factor scores on factor H—neither group is unusual on the size-wealth dimension. Note that the Soviet Union, the United States, and China are at the very top of the graph, but exhibit very different scores on factor H.

Differences between the Two factor Analyses

One reason for including both tables 3-3 and 3-4 was to get an indication of the effect of the nonmarine variables. It can be argued that comparing the results of the two tables would give one a measure of the importance of marine attributes in comparison to the whole range of national characteristics. Table 3-5 highlights this comparison for factors A and 9. These two factors were selected because they identify identical patterns. Otherwise one might confuse the importance of marine variables with a change or redistribution in the way the factor analysis isolates the general patterns. It is reasonable to infer that the major difference between the factors will come from the deletion of the nonmarine variables. Table 3-5 contains the factor scores for the total data matrix, the marine variables-only matrix, and the difference between the two. The differences between the "marine" and "total" columns have been signed to indicate whether the omission of nonmarine elements increased or decreased the country's magnitude on the factor. States included are the five examined in chapter 2 and several others selected for comparative purposes.

Table 3-5 shows that for about half of the countries the change from the total data matrix to the marine-only matrix did not have a significant effect—Belguim, China, France, the Philippines, and the Soviet Union fall in this category.

Table 3-5
Comparison of Factor Scores — Factor A and Factor 9

Country	Factor A Size-Wealth	Factor 9 Marine Size-Wealth	Difference
Australia	−.71	− .36	+ .35
Belgium	−.67	− .68	− .01
Canada	−.78	− .30	+ .48
China	2.57	2.65	+ .08
Denmark	−.54	− .29	+ .25
France	.09	.04	− .05
Iceland	−.41	− .15	+ .26
Iran	.44	− .07	− .51
Nigeria	.08	− .41	− .49
Philippines	−.36	− .51	− .15
USSR	9.86	10.02	+ .16
US	4.45	2.49	−1.96

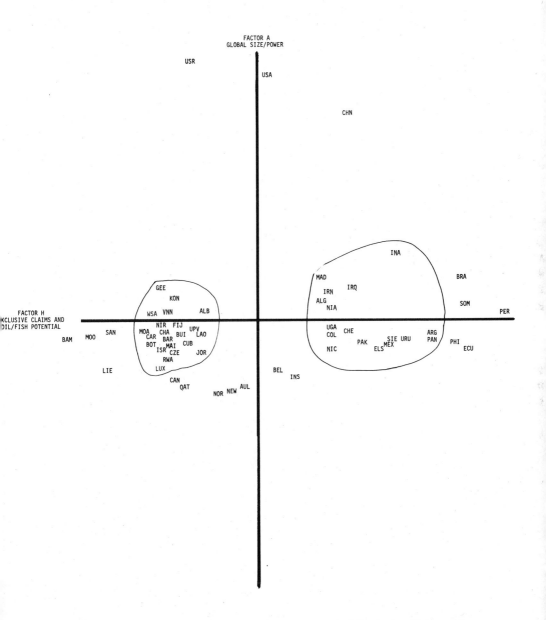

Figure 3-10. Relationship between Global Size-Power and Exclusive Claims and Oil-Fish Potential

It must be remembered that this does not mean marine things are unimportant to these countries, only that restricting the analysis to marine variables does not produce significant changes. Clearly the largest single change is the United States. The United States scores very highly on both factor A and factor 9, but when the analysis is limited to marine variables, the United States loses ground. It should be remembered, however, that the United States score of 2.49 is still second highest in the world.

For Australia, Canada, Denmark, and Iceland, limiting the analysis to marine variables has produced moderately strong increases in the factor scores suggesting high levels of marine importance. In the case of Canada this would seem to be consistent with the results of chapter 2. Iran and Nigeria show significant decreases when the nonmarine characteristics are eliminated. In both cases the changes are pronounced. Iran's score drops from considerably above average to below average. Nigeria moves from about average to much below average. These results indicate that the elements of wealth and power in these two states, at least for the present, come mainly from nonmarine sources. Again this seems consistent with the findings of chapter 2. It would be insightful to look for trends if these factor scores were computed again five years from now.

Conclusions

This section has taken a general approach to the problem of marine policy. The premise here has been that a general model containing some 90 variables can describe adequately the marine policy of most of the countries of the world. The attempt has been largely successful. Countries' marine policies seem to fall along fewer than ten broad dimensions. These dimensions relate to size-wealth, relative coastal importance, absolute coastal size, oil resources, acceptance of the 1958 Geneva Conventions, shipping-fishing importance, and zonal size-zonal claims. In combination, these factors seem to provide a sensitive, accurate picture of the marine policies of countries.

Another important finding is that those elements of the model called processing do not seem to have much impact on marine policies. From this one might logically infer that many of the things preoccupying political scientists, for example, degree of political competition, have little direct bearing on marine policy. It is tempting to assert that marine policies often have clear-cut resource or strategic components that transcend political ideological differences. This would seem to be substantiated by the posture similarity of countries with very different political systems, for example, the United States and the Soviet Union.

Appendix 3A

Variables and the Model

Table 3A-1
Variables and the Model

Variable Name	Units	Explanation	Mean	Standard Deviation	Examples Name	Value	Source
Inputs (Nonmarine)							
I1 LAND AREA	km²		905,754	2,490,372	First: USSR Top quarter: SOMALI Median: OMAN Bottom quarter: DOMREP Last: MONACO	22,274,910 637,660 212,460 48,730 3	Forstall, Richard L. (ed.), *1973 Commercial Atlas and Marketing Guide*, 104th ed. Chicago: Rand McNally & Co., 1973.
I2 ARABLE LAND	Percent	The percentage excludes areas unfit for food production and forested or developed regions.	19	17	First: TONGA Top quarter: NEPAL Median: DAHOME Bottom quarter: NICARA Last: MAURIA	71 18 14 6 0	*Britannica World Atlas International*, 1966. Encyclopaedia Britannica, Inc. *Oxford Economic Atlas of the World*, 4th ed., Oxford University Press, 1972 *Rand McNally Cosmopolitan World Atlas*, New York: Rand McNally & Co., 1958.
I3 OIL RESERVES (Ultimate Onshore)	Scale 1 = high 7 = low	Expressed on a scale from 1 to 7: 1 = 1,000-10,000 billion barrels	4.9	1.6	First: USSR(7)[a] Top Quarter:	2	*Summary Petroleum and Selected Mineral Statistics for 120 Countries, Including Offshore Areas,*

2 = 100-1,000 billion barrels
3 = 10-100 billion barrels
4 = 1-10 billion barrels
5 = 0.1-1 billion barrels
6 = 0.01-0.1 billion barrels
7 = <0.01 billion barrels

		ROMANI (39)	4	U.S. Geological Survey, Professional Paper 817, 1973
		Median:		
		BELGIM (28)	5	
		Bottom quarter:		
		CHAD (40)	7	
		Last:		
		TONGA (40)	7	
I4 OIL RESERVES (Proven Onshore)	Millions metric tons			
		First:		*Summary of 1972 Oil and Gas Statistics for Onshore and Offshore Areas of 151 Countries.* U.S. Geological Survey, Professional Paper 885, 1974.
	448	SAUDIA	11,500	
	1,638	Top quarter:		
		PERU	33	
		Median:		
		SUDAN (87)	0	
		Bottom quarter:		
		SRLNKA (87)	0	
		Last:		
		MONGOL (87)	0	
I5 ARABLE LAND × LAND AREA		First:		
		USSR	2,227,491	
		Top quarter:		
		IRAQ	69,589	
	98,356	Median:		
	294,298	LIBERI	22,274	
		Bottom quarter:		
		SWITZD	4,542	
		Last:		
		MONACO (3)	0	
Inputs (Marine)				
I6 SEABED AREA (200 Meters)	km²	The 200-meter isobath has been the traditional		
	86,123	First:		*Limits in the Seas: Theoretical Areal.*
	147,812	CANADA	1,653,215	

[a]In case of ties, denotes number in the group with same score.

Table 3A-1—*Continued*

Variable Name	Units	Explanation	Mean	Standard Deviation	Examples		Source
					Name	Value	
		legal definition of the continental shelf as put forth in the 1958 Geneva Convention.			Top quarter: CUBA	45,505	*Allocations of Seabed to Coastal States.* International Boundary Study, U.S. Dept. of State, Series A, No. 4, 1973.
					Median: CHILE	15,624	
					Bottom quarter: BELGIM	1,562	
					Last: BOTSWA (27)	0	
I7 SEABED AREA (3,000 Meters)	km²	The 3,000-meter isobath has traditionally marked the legal extent of the continental margin.	185,347	438,778	First: AUSTRA	2,822,866	*Limits in the Seas: Theoretical Areal Allocations of Seabed to Coastal States.*
					Top quarter: PHILIP	126,945	
					Median: GHANA	39,255	
					Bottom quarter: NAURU	3,910	
					Last: MALI (27)	0	
I8 SEABED AREA (200 Miles)	km²	The 200-mile limit has generally been accepted as the boundary for coastal states' economic zones.	325,094	705,471	First: US	4,339,566	(Same as above, I7)
					Top quarter: GREECE	287,677	
					Median: KORE.N	73,827	
					Bottom quarter: SYRIA	5,859	

Last:
LAOS (27) — 0

Sovereignty of the Sea. State Department, Geographic Bulletin, No. 3, 1969.

Variable	Units	Mean	S.D.	Distribution	Source
I9 SHORELINE LENGTH	km	4,103	11,774	First: CANADA — 104,564 Top quarter: VIET.S — 3,054 Median: URUGUA — 759 Bottom quarter: DAHOME — 139 Last: AUSTRI (26) — 0	Sovereignty of the Sea. State Department, Geographic Bulletin, No. 3, 1969.
I10 OIL RESERVES (Ultimate Offshore)	Scale = 1 = high, 7 = low. Expressed on a scale from 1 to 7: 1 = 1,000–10,000 billion barrels 2 = 100–1,000 billion barrels 3 = 10–100 billion barrels 4 = 1–10 billion barrels 5 = 0.1–1 billion barrels 6 = 0.01–0.1 billion barrels 7 = <0.01 billion barrels	5.0	1.5	First: LIBYA (5) — 2 Top quarter: CYPRUS (45) — 4 Median: SINGAP (32) — 5 Bottom quarter: BOLIVI (44) — 7 Last: ICELAN (44) — 7	Summary Petroleum and Selected Mineral Statistics for 120 Countries, Including Offshore Areas.
I11 OIL RESERVES (Proven Offshore)	Millions metric tons	136	808	First: SAUDIA — 7,879 Top quarter: FIJI (117) — 0 Median: FRANCE (117) — 0 Bottom quarter: ELSALV (117) — 0 Last: PARAGU (117) — 0	(Same as above, I10) Summary of 1972 Oil and Gas Statistics for Onshore And Offshore Areas of 151 Countries.

Table 3A-1—*Continued*

Variable Name	Units	Explanation	Mean	Standard Deviation	Examples		Source
					Name	*Value*	
112 SEMIENCLOSED SEAS BORDERED	Number	The following 25 water bodies are considered to be semienclosed seas: 1. Gulf of Aden 2. Andaman Sea 3. Baffin Bay-Davis Strait 4. Baltic Sea 5. Bering Sea 6. Bismarck Sea 7. Black Sea 8. Caribbean Sea 9. Celebes Sea 10. East China-Yellow Seas 11. Hudson Bay 12. Sea of Japan 13. Java-Flores-Banda Seas 14. Kara Sea 15. Mediterranean Sea 16. Gulf of Mexico 17. North Sea 18. Sea of Okhotsk 19. Persian Gulf 20. Red Sea 21. Gulf of St. Lawrence 22. Solomon Sea	0.75	1.01	First: USSR (2) Top quarter: TRIN.T (53) Median: JORDAN (53) Bottom quarter: ZAMBIA (69) Last: CHAD (69)	6 1 1 0 0	Alexander, Lewis M., "Regionalism and the Law of the Sea: The Case of Semienclosed Seas," *Ocean Development and International Law 2,* No. 2 (Summer 1974), 151-186.

Variable	Units	Description	Mean	Distribution	Reference
23. South China Sea 24. Sulu Sea 25. Timor-Arafura Seas		This variable gives the number of these seas on which each state borders.	1.35	First: INDONS Top quarter: NEWZEA (22) Median: BELGIM (101) Bottom quarter: SWITZD (101) Last: LAOS	
I13 INTERNATIONAL STRAITS BORDERED	Number	Sixty-three straits used for international transit were considered. This variable gives the number of international straits on which each state borders.	.59	11 1 0 0 0	Smith, Robert W., *An Analysis of the Concept "Strategic Quality of International Straits:" A Geographical Perspective with Focus on Petroleum Tanker Transit and on the Malacca Strait.* University of Rhode Island, 1973.
I14 FISH POTENTIAL WITHIN 200 MILES (%)	% highly productive area in economic zone	Little quantitative information is available on maximum sustainable yields for most of the world and what estimates exist are refuted by many experts. For this reason the parameter of phytoplankton production was chosen as being indicative of fish stocks. Areas where phytoplankton production exceeds 250 milligrams of carbon per square meter per day are taken to be areas of high fishery potential. This variable designates the			*Oxford Economic Atlas of the World*, Map, Global Aspects of Marine Fisheries," information source FAO and Office of the Geographer, Department of State, 1974.

Table 3A-1–*Continued*

Variable Name	Units	Explanation	Mean	Standard Deviation	Examples		Source
					Name	*Value*	
I15 SEABED 200 METERS LAND AREA		percentage of highly productive area of the state's total 200-mile zone.	1.53	8.83	First: NAURU	97.65	
					Top quarter: HONDUR	.27	
					Median: GUINEA	.09	
					Bottom quarter: CAMRON	.01	
					Last: BOTSWA (27)	0	
I16 SEABED 3,000 METERS LAND AREA			6.42	35.46	First: TONGA	334.91	
					Top quarter: QATAR	.62	
					Median: MOROCO	.18	
					Bottom quarter: ETHIOP	.04	
					Last: LUXEMB (27)	0	

I17	SEABED 200 MILES LAND AREA	50.1	363.5		
				First: NAURU	3906.00
				Top quarter: NETHER	1.32
				Median: COLOMB	.30
				Bottom quarter: ETHIOP	.04
				Last: MONACO (27)	0

I18	SEABED 3,000 METERS SEABED 200 METERS	3.31	4.04		
				First: TONGA	28.58
				Top quarter: LIBERI	3.44
				Median: GUATEM	2.28
				Bottom quarter: YUGOSL	1.43
				Last: ZAIRE (18)	1.00

I19	SEABED 200 MILES SEABED 200 METERS	16.7	68.7		
				First: FIJI	551.40
				Top quarter: GUATEM	8.00
				Median: ITALY	3.80
				Bottom quarter: ARGENT	1.50
				Last: ZAIRE (18)	1.00

Table 3A-1–*Continued*

Variable Name	Units	Explanation	Mean	Standard Deviation	Examples		Source
					Name	*Value*	
I20 SHORELINE LENGTH / LAND AREA			0.073	.299	First: MALDIV	2.467	
					Top quarter: NORWAY	.021	
					Median: URUGUA	.004	
					Bottom quarter: ETHIOP	.001	
					Last: BOTSWA (26)	0	
I21 OIL OFF ULTIMATE / OIL ON ULTIMATE			1.06	.33	First: NORWAY (2)	.429	
					Top quarter: MALAWI (86)	1.000	
					Median: SYEMEN (86)	1.000	
					Bottom quarter: BARBDO (86)	1.000	
					Last: ALGERI	3.500	
I22 HIGH FISH POTEN. × SEABED 200 MILES			$1{,}437 \times 10^4$	$3{,}316 \times 10^4$	First: US	$21{,}697 \times 10^4$	
					Top quarter: GABON	$1{,}217 \times 10^4$	
					Median: MOROCO	238×10^4	

Processing Section

	Scale / Units	Description					
P1 DEGREE POLITICAL COMPETITION	Scale: 3 = high 1 = low	A scale of 1-3 gives a measure of internal political competition: 3 = high competition, open political-party system 2 = medium competition, limited opposition tolerated 1 = low competition, one-party, absolutist systems	1.8	0.7	Bottom quarter: MALTA (49) Last: CHAD (49)	26 – "3s" – High 64 – "2s" – Med 52 – "1s" – Low	0 0
P2 GEOGRAPHIC REGION	1-6	1 = Western Europe and English speaking 2 = Latin America 3 = East Europe and USSR (Soviet Bloc) 4 = Middle East 5 = Central and Southern Africa 6 = South and East Asia					
P3 YEARS OF INDEPENDENCE	Number of years	If a state has been independent for more than 200 years, it is given the value 200. The time dates back from 1975.	76.5	73.7			

Taylor, Charles L., and Hudson, Michael C. (eds.) *World Handbook of Political and Social Indicators*, 2nd ed. New Haven: Yale Univ. Press, 1972.

Table 3A-1–*Continued*

Variable Name	Units	Explanation	Mean	Standard Deviation	Examples Name	Value	Source
P4 AGE OF CONSTITUTION	Number of years	The age dates back from 1975.	31.6	41.5			The Official Associated Press Almanac 1973. (Same as above, P3)
Outputs (Nonmarine)							
O1 LITERACY RATE	Percent	Because literacy is a subjectively defined quantity, and may be measured differently among different states (or only estimated), this variable expresses only approximate relative differences among states.	57	33	First: JAPAN (22) Top quarter: ROMANI (2) Median: MALDIV Bottom quarter: OMAN (7) Last: NIGER	99 92 58 25 4	1973 UNESCO Statistical Yearbook. 1965 UNESCO Statistical Yearbook. Russett, Bruce M. et al. (eds.). World Handbook of Political and Social Indicators. New Haven: Yale Univ. Press, 1964. World Handbook of Political and Social Indicators, 2nd ed. The Official Associated Press Almanac 1973.
O2 POPULATION	Thousands	Values are for 1974.	26,961	89,611	First: CHINA Top quarter: SUDAN Median: GUATEM	827,780 17,320 5,690	1975 Information Please Almanac Atlas and Yearbook. New York: Doubleday & Co. 1973 U.N. Statistical Yearbook.

					Bottom quarter: NICARA	2,035
					Last: NAURU	7
O3	POPULATION GROWTH RATE	Percent	Values are averaged over several years. Growth rates are subject to relatively rapid fluctuations reflecting changing social and economic conditions.	2.2	1.2	
					First: KUWAIT	9.8
					Top quarter: RWANDA	2.9
					Median: CAMBOD	2.3
					Bottom quarter: ICELAN	1.3
					Last: GERM.E (2)	0
						World Handbook of Political and Social Indicators, 2nd ed.
O4	GROSS NATIONAL PRODUCT	Millions US $	Values are for 1972.	24,622	102,434	
					First: US	1,100,431
					Top quarter: PHILIP	9,691
					Median: LEBNON	1,903
					Bottom quarter: UPVOLT	405
					Last: MALDIV	13
						World Bank Atlas, 1973. IBRD.
O5	SCIENCE MANPOWER	Number	This variable includes the number of scientists and engineers engaged in research and development.	14,528	81,826	
					First: USSR	806,300
					Top quarter: AUSTRI	2,040
					Median: LAOS	140
						1971 UNESCO Statistical Yearbook.

Table 3A-1—*Continued*

					Examples		
Variable Name	*Units*	*Explanation*	*Mean*	*Standard Deviation*	*Name*	*Value*	*Source*
					Bottom quarter: DOMREP (9)	20	
					Last: LIECHT (3)	0	
O6 OIL PRODUCTION ONSHORE	10^6 metric tons		15.4	57.4	First: US	403	*Summary of 1972 Oil and Gas Statistics for Onshore and Offshore Areas of 151 Countries.*
					Top quarter: HUNGAR (7)	2	
					Median: SENEGL (97)	0	
					Bottom quarter: JAMAIC (97)	0	
					Last: AFGHAN (97)	0	
O7 BILATERAL TREATIES (Number of)	Number		212	384	First: US	3,402	Gamble, John K., and Fischer, Dana D., *The ICJ: An Analysis of a Failure.* Lexington: D.C. Heath and Co., 1976.
					Top quarter: U.A.R.	237	
					Median: ALGERI (2)	83	
					Bottom quarter: UGANDA (2)	37	
					Last: GUYANA (9)	0	

O8	MULTILATERAL TREATIES (Number of)	Number	70	65	First: FRANCE — 307 Top quarter: HAITI — 87 Median: NIGERI — 53 Bottom quarter: SANMAR (2) — 25 Last: SYEMEN (12) — 0	Gamble and Fischer, *The ICJ: An Analysis of a Failure.*
O9	INTERNAT'L ORGAN. (No. Member of)	Number 10 max. 10 poss.	8.3	2.4	First: FRANCE (54) — 10 Top quarter: SPAIN (54) — 10 Median: NIGER (38) — 9 Bottom quarter: BURUND (25) — 8 Last: TONGA (2) — 0	*Yearbook of International Organizations*, 15th ed. Brussels: Union of International Associations, 1974.

Value gives membership in the following ten organizations:

1. International Labor Organization
2. Food and Agricultural Organization
3. U.N. Educational, Scientific, and Cultural Organization
4. World Health Organization
5. International Bank for Reconstruction and Development
6. International Civil Aviation Organization
7. International Telecommunication Union
8. World Meteorological Organization

Table 3A-1—*Continued*

Variable Name	Units	Explanation	Mean	Standard Deviation	Examples Name	Examples Value	Source
		9. Inter-Governmental Maritime Consultative Organization 10. International Atomic Energy Agency					
O10 DISPUTE SETTLEMENT TREATIES	Number	The value is the number of treaties since World War II to which each state is a party containing dispute-settlement clauses.	45.3	46.9	First: US Top quarter: PERU Median: PARAGU (4) Bottom quarter: DAHOME (8) Last: FIJI (15)	233 53 31 14 0	Gamble and Fischer, *The ICJ: An Analysis of a Failure.*
O11 ICJ USE TREATIES	Number	The value is the number of treaties since World War II to which each state is a party containing a dispute-settlement clause calling for use of the International Court of Justice.	8.37	8.39	First: US Top quarter: LIBERI (7) Median: COSTA (11) Bottom quarter: SINGA (8) Last: LESOTH (26)	43 12 6 3 0	(Same as above, O10)

Variable	Units / Scale	Description			Distribution	Source
O12 ICJ SUP-PORT	Scale: 9 = high 1 = low	Index of total support of International Court of Justice combining appearance before the Court and acceptance of the Optional Clause.	2.79	1.42	First: UK — 9; Top quarter: CANADA (22) — 3; Median: ALGERI (79) — 2; Bottom quarter: GABON (79) — 2; Last: KORE.N (9) — 1	(Same as above, O10)
O13 COPPER PRODUCTION	Thousands metric tons	Annual copper production.	44.5	175.0	First: US — 1,381; Top quarter: AUSTRI (3) — 3; Median: GAMBIA (85) — 0; Bottom quarter: NEPAL (85) — 0; Last: BARBDO (85) — 0	1972 U.N. Statistical Yearbook
O14 NICKEL PRODUCTION	Thousands metric tons	Annual nickel production.	3.67	24.8	First: CANADA — 267; Top quarter: CZECHK (129) — 0; Median: LUXEMB (129) — 0; Bottom quarter: NEPAL (129) — 0; Last: TONGA (129) — 0	1972 U.N. Statistical Yearbook
O15 MANGANESE PRODUCTION	Thousands metric tons	Annual manganese production.	57.9	278.4	First: USSR — 2,552; Top quarter: POLAND (110) — 0	1972 U.N. Statistical Yearbook

Table 3A-1—Continued

Variable Name	Units	Explanation	Mean	Standard Deviation	Examples Name	Value	Source
					Median:		
					CAMBOD (110)	0	
					Bottom quarter:		
					SENEGL (110)	0	
					Last:		
					BAHAMA (110)	0	
016 COBALT PRO-DUCTION	Thousands metric tons	Annual cobalt production.	0.17	1.14	First:		1971 Minerals Yearbook, Vol. 1, U.S. Bureau of Mines, p. 409.
					ZAIRE	13	
					Top quarter:		
					FRANCE (133)	0	
					Median:		
					CAMBOD (133)	0	
					Bottom quarter:		
					TUNISI (133)	0	
					Last:		
					OMAN (133)	0	
017 POPULATION AREA			50.1	363.5	First:		
					MONACO	8.667	
					Top quarter:		
					DENMRK	.118	
					Median:		
					SYRIA	.038	
					Bottom quarter:		
					CHILE	.014	
					Last:		
					MONGOL	.001	

O18	GNP / POPULATION	3.31	4.04	First: US 5.193
				Top quarter: ARGENT 1.222
				Median: IRAQ .365
				Bottom quarter: TOGO .149
				Last: RWANDA .061
O19	SCIENTISTS / POPULATION	16.7	68.7	First: USSR 3.200
				Top quarter: SAFRIC .170
				Median: IRAN .035
				Bottom quarter: GHANA .011
				Last: NAURU (3) 0

Outputs (Marine)

O20	RESEARCH VESSELS	Number	2.4	11.6	First: USSR 108
					Top quarter: QATAR (107) 0
					Median: SUDAN (107) 0
					Bottom quarter: CAMRON (107) 0
					Last: MALTA (107) 0

Lloyd's Register of Shipping Statistical Tables, 1973.

Table 3A-1–*Continued*

Variable Name	Units	Explanation	Mean	Standard Deviation	Examples		Source
					Name	*Value*	
O21 NAVAL VESSELS (Large)	Number	These ships have offensive capabilities.	11.8	49.2	First: USSR	481	*Jane's Fighting Ships, 1973-1974.*
					Top quarter: IRAN (2)	7	
					Median: NICARA (88)	0	
					Bottom quarter: SOMALI (88)	0	
					Last: BARBDO (88)	0	
O22 NAVAL VESSELS (Coastal)	Number	These vessels are primarily defensive and operate near to states' coasts.	29.7	71.0	First: CHINA	590	*Jane's Fighting Ships, 1973-1974.*
					Top quarter: IRAN (2)	34	
					Median: JAMAIC (4)	6	
					Bottom quarter: RWANDA (44)	0	
					Last: HUNGAR (44)	0	
O23 SUBMARINES	Number		5.8	35.1	First: USSR	396	*Jane's Fighting Ships, 1973-1974.*
					Top quarter: BURMA (107)	0	
					Median: JAMAIC (107)	0	

Variable	Units	Description	Mean	S.D.	Statistics	Source
					Bottom quarter: BAHRAI (107) 0 Last: AUSTRI 0	
O24 MERCHANT SHIPPING TONNAGE	Gross tons	This variable gives the tonnage of vessels registered in each state. Because the owners of many vessels are of states other than the flag state (i.e., many owners register under "flags of convenience"), this figure may be misleading for some states.	1,868,858	6,261,228	First: LIBERI 49,696,293 Top quarter: INDONS 593,603 Median: BURMA 46,927 Bottom quarter: BAHRAI 1,877 Last: LUXEMB (27) 0	Lloyd's Register of Shipping, 1973.
O25 SHIPBUILDING	Gross tons	Values are for 1972. Values not given in Lloyd's were extrapolated from values given for earlier years in the Oxford Economic Atlas of the World.	192,218	1,114,126	First: JAPAN 12,857,119 Top quarter: SAFRIC 2,000 Median: AFGHAN (97) 0 Bottom quarter: TONGA (97) 0 Last: BURUND (97) 0	Lloyd's Register of Shipping Statistical Tables, 1973. Oxford Economic Atlas of the World.
O26 SEABORNE TRADE	Thousands metric tons	Values include both imports and exports.	34,108	76,132	First: US 511,042 Top quarter: KORE.S 22,720 Median: IVORYC 5,697 Bottom quarter: DAHOME 561 Last: NEPAL (28) 0	U.N. Statistical Yearbook, 1972.

Table 3A-1–Continued

Variable Name	Units	Explanation	Mean	Standard Deviation	Examples		Source
					Name	Value	
O27 FISH CATCH	Thousands metric tons	Annual fish catch.	421	1,407	First: PERU	10,661	1971 Yearbook of Fisheries Statistics.
					Top quarter: MOROCO (2)	299	
					Median: ISRAEL (2)	28	
					Bottom quarter: BAHAMA (4)	2	
					Last: LESOTH (32)	0	
O28 FISH IMPORTS	Thousands US $	Values are for 1970. Values for some states are derived from tonnage imported.	23,148	83,886	First: US	835,781	1973 FAO Yearbook of Fisheries Statistics, Vol. 37.
					Top quarter: SAFRIC	10,338	
					Median: MAURIT	993	
					Bottom quarter: INDIA	64	
					Last: SANMAR (28)	0	
O29 FISH EXPORTS	Thousands US $	Values are for 1970. Values for some states are derived from tonnage exported figures.	19,517	54,598	First: PERU	339,228	1973 FAO Yearbook of Fisheries Statistics, Vol. 37.
					Top quarter: YUGOSL	8,832	
					Median: SWITZD	716	

Variable	Units			Description	Distribution	Value	Source
					Bottom quarter: GHANA (36)	0	
					Last: MONGOL (36)	0	
O30 OIL PRODUCTION (Offshore)	10^6 Metric tons	2.1	10.8		First: SAUDIA	103	*Summary of 1972 Oil and Gas Statistics for Onshore and Offshore Areas of 151 Countries.*
					Top quarter: ARGENT (125)	0	
					Median: IRAQ (125)	0	
					Bottom quarter: GUATEM (125)	0	
					Last: OMAN (125)	0	
O31 SEAFOOD CONSUMPTION PER CAPITA	Calories per day	20	23	Per-capita seafood intake	First: ICELAN	117	*FAO Production Yearbook,* Vol. 25, 1971.
					Top quarter: CHILE (4)	28	
					Median: MALTA	13	
					Bottom quarter: SUDAN (4)	2	
					Last: BANGLA (27)	0	
O32 FISHERY COMMISSION MEMBERSHIP	Number	1.4	2.1	This variable gives the number of commissions of which a state is a member: 1. Regional Fisheries Advisory Commission for the South-West Atlantic 2. Fishery Commission for the Eastern Central Atlantic	First: JAPAN	12	
					Top quarter: INDIA (15)	2	
					Median: URUGUA (45)	1	
					Bottom quarter: FIJI (59)	0	
					Last: HUNGAR (59)	0	

Table 3A-1–*Continued*

Variable Name	Units	Explanation	Mean	Standard Deviation	Examples		Source
					Name	*Value*	
		3. General Fisheries Council for the Mediterranean					
		4. Indian Ocean Fisheries Commission					
		5. Indo-Pacific Fisheries Council					
		6. International Commission for the Northwest Atlantic Fisheries					
		7. International Commission for the Southeast Atlantic Fisheries					
		8. International North Pacific Fisheries Commission					
		9. Japan-Republic of Korea Joint Fisheries Commission					
		10. Japanese-Soviet Fisheries Commission for the Northwest Pacific					
		11. Mixed Commission for Black Sea Fisheries					
		12. Northeast Atlantic Fisheries Commission					
		13. Permanent Commission of the Conference on					

the Use of Marine Resources of the South Pacific
14. Baltic Sea Salmon Standing Committee
15. Inter-American Tropical Tuna Commission
16. International Commission for the Conservation of Atlantic Tuna
17. International Pacific Halibut Commission

Variable	Coding	Description	Mean	S.D.	Distribution	N	Source
O33 UN LOS CONFERENCE DELEGATION	Number	This variable includes all listed members of the delegation.	10.2	12.9	First: US; Top quarter: ICELAN (8); Median: SIERRA (17); Bottom quarter: ZAMBIA (17); Last: BURUND (7)	111, 11, 6, 4, 0	U.N. Delegate list – Delegations to the Third United Nations Conference on the Law of the Sea – Fourth Session, Doc. A/CONF. 62/INF.5, 12 April 1976.
O34 IOC MEMBERSHIP	1 = Yes 0 = No	International Oceanographic Commission membership as of December, 1975.	.58	.50			December, 1975 U.N. List.
O35 SCOR MEMBERSHIP	Number	Scientific Committee on Oceanic Research membership. This is a nongovernmental committee. As such this variable gives the number of	.75	1.68	First: US; Top quarter: IRELAN (110); Median: COLOMB (110)	10, 0, 0	SCOR Proceedings Supplement June 1975. London: International Council of Scientific Unions, October 1975.

Table 3A-1—*Continued*

Variable Name	Units	Explanation	Mean	Standard Deviation	Examples Name	Examples Value	Source
		citizens of each state who are members of the committee.			Bottom quarter: UPVOLT (110) Last: NAURU (110)	0 0	Alexander, Lewis, "Indices of National Interest in the Oceans," *Ocean Development and International Law* 1, No. 1 (Spring 1973).
O36 U.N. SEABED COMMITTEE		1 = Yes 0 = No	.62	.49			
O37 '58 TERRITORIAL SEA CONVENTION	Scale: 1-4	This variable tells what relationship, if any, the state has with the 1958 Geneva Conventions. A scale is used as follows: 1-No obligation 2-Signature not followed by necessary ratification 3-Some kind of reservation or qualification plus ratification 4-full, unqualified ratification	1.92	1.22			
O38 '58 CONTINENTAL SHELF CONVENTION	Scale: 1-4	(Same as above, O37)	2.13	1.33			

039 '58 HIGH SEAS CON-VENTION	Scale: 1-4	(Same as above, O37)	2.10	1.29	
040 '58 FISHER-IES CONVEN-TION	Scale: 1-4	This variable tells what relationship, if any, the state has with the 1958 Geneva Conventions. A scale is used as follows: 1–No obligation 2–Signature not followed by necessary ratification 3–Some kind of reserva-tion or qualification plus ratification 4–full, unqualified ratification	1.83	1.22	
041 IMCO OIL POLLUTION CONVENTIONS	Scale: 1-3	The International Con-vention for the Pre-vention of Pollution of the Sea by Oil was signed in 1954 and entered into force in 1958. Amend-ments to parts of the original Convention entered into force in 1967. Important new amendments were adopted at the IMCO meeting of October 21, 1969. A scale was used as follows to describe status:	1.45	.68	American Society of International Law. Final Act of the International Legal Conference on Marine Pollution Damage, 1969. *International Legal Materials* 9 (January 1970).

Table 3A-1—*Continued*

Variable Name	Units	Explanation	Mean	Standard Deviation	Examples			Source
					Name	Value		
		1 – No action on either the original Convention or 1969 amendments						
		2 – Ratified the 1954 Convention or signed the 1969 amendments						
		3 – Ratified the 1954 Convention and signed the 1969 amendments						
O42 TERRITORIAL SEA WIDTH	Nautical miles		24.6	54.2	First: PHILIP	300		*Limits in the Seas No. 36 – National Claims to Maritime Jurisdiction.* Revised December 23, 1975. The Geographer, Office of the Geographer, Bureau of Intelligence and Research.
					Top quarter: LIBYA (54)	12		
					Median: SAMOA (54)	12		
					Bottom quarter: SINGAP (25)	3		
					Last: MALAWI (27)	0		
O43 FISHERIES ZONE WIDTH	Nautical miles		37.6	65.6	First: PHILIP	300		(Same as above, O42)
					Top quarter: FRANCE (67)	12		
					Median: MAURIT (67)	12		

Code & Name	Scale / Description			Statistics		Source
044 ECONOMIC ZONE RE-STRICTIVE-NESS	Scale: 6 = Restrictive 1 = Free	A scale of 1-6 describes each state's view on the extent of national jurisdiction over the 200-mile economic zone as expressed at the Caracas session of the U.N.'s Third Conference on the Law of the Sea. As many different views are possible and not necessarily linear, the values are somewhat subjective. On the scale, 6 is most restrictive and 1 is least restrictive.	3.18	1.55	Bottom quarter: GERM.W (11) — 3 Last: SANMAR (25) — 0	Modified from information from Miles, Edward. "An Interpretation of the Caracas Proceedings," *Law of the Sea: Caracas and Beyond*. Christy et al. (eds.). Cambridge: Ballinger, 1975.
045 PROVEN OFF OIL / GNP			.047	.243	First: SAUDIA — 1.801 Top quarter: ISRAEL (117) — 0 Median: MAURIT (117) — 0 Bottom quarter: CAMRON (117) — 0 Last: BELGIM (117) — 0	
046 RESEARCH VESSELS / GNP			0.00016	0.00077	First: BAHAMA — .00655	

Table 3A-1—*Continued*

Variable Name	Units	Explanation	Mean	Standard Deviation	Examples Name	Value	Source
					Top quarter: NAURU (107)	0	
					Median: ALBANI (107)	0	
					Bottom quarter: BOTSWA (107)	0	
					Last: BURUND (107)	0	
047 RESEARCH VESSELS SHORELINE LENGTH			0.0011	0.0041	First: IRAQ	0.0299	
					Top quarter: BRAZIL	0.0001	
					Median: BAHRAI (81)	0	
					Bottom quarter: MOROCO (81)	0	
					Last: SOMALI (81)	0	
048 RESEARCH VESSELS NO. SCIENTISTS			0.0043	0.0306	First: BAHAMA	.30000	
					Top quarter: CHINA	.00004	
					Median: DOMREP (104)	0	

		Bottom quarter: SYEMEN (104)			0
		Last: RWANDA (104)			0
O49 RESEARCH VESSELS NAVAL VESSELS	.075	.264	First: LIBERI	2.000
			Top quarter: BULGAR	.030
			Median: URUGUA (63)	0
			Bottom quarter: ECUADR (63)	0
			Last: SOMALI (63)	0
O50 LARGE NAVAL VESSELS COASTAL NAVAL VESSELS	.339	.640	First: CANADA	4.571
			Top quarter: DOMREP	.438
			Median: SYRIA	.071
			Bottom quarter: NICARA (42)	0
			Last: ETHIOP (42)	0
O51 NAVAL VESSELS GNP	.00497	.00801	First: SOMALI	.04608
			Top quarter: PERU	.00552
			Median: SAUDIA	.00229

Table 3A-1–*Continued*

					Examples		
Variable Name	*Units*	*Explanation*	*Mean*	*Standard Deviation*	*Name*	*Value*	*Source*
					Bottom quarter: CONGO (44)	0	
					Last: SANMAR (44)	0	
O52 $\dfrac{\text{NAVAL VESSELS}}{\text{POPULATION}}$			.00277	.00451	First: ICELAN	.02273	
					Top quarter: URUGUA	.00331	
					Median: SAFRIC	.00119	
					Bottom quarter: CONGO (44)	0	
					Last: NAURU (44)	0	
O53 $\dfrac{\text{COASTAL NAVAL VESSELS}}{\text{200-MILE ZONE AREA}}$			0.00222	0.01144	First: IRAQ	.09463	
					Top quarter: CAMBOD	.00032	
					Median: PORTGL	.00007	
					Bottom quarter: SIERRA	.00001	
					Last: ZAIRE	0	

O54 __SHIPPING FLAG TONNAGE__ 1,233 11,839
    GNP

First:
LIBERI 140,783
Top quarter:
GHANA 51
Median:
SUDAN 19
Bottom quarter:
GUATEM 4
Last:
LIECHT (27) 0

O55 __SHIPPING FLAG TONNAGE__ 152 672
    SEABORNE TRADE

First:
MALDIV 5,920
Top quarter:
CHINA 35
Median:
CANADA 12
Bottom quarter:
GUYANA 2
Last:
DAHOME (9) 0

O56 __SHIPBUILDING__ 2.98 10.47
    GNP

First:
NORWAY 64.64
Top quarter:
KORE.N .31
Median:
IRAQ (97) 0
Bottom quarter:
ALBANI (97) 0
Last:
MALI (97) 0

Table 3A-1—*Continued*

Variable Name	Units	Explanation	Mean	Standard Deviation	Examples		Source
					Name	*Value*	
O57 SEABORNE TRADE / GNP			7.07	15.46	First: NAURU	80.18	
					Top quarter: GUINEA	4.17	
					Median: TONGA	1.88	
					Bottom quarter: GERM.W	.62	
					Last: RWANDA (28)	0	
O58 FISH CATCH / GNP			0.0594	0.1856	First: PERU	1.5403	
					Top quarter: PANAMA	.0447	
					Median: NETHER	.0088	
					Bottom quarter: IRAN	.0016	
					Last: MALAWI (32)	0	
O59 FISH CATCH / FISH POTENTIAL W/I 200 MILES			960×10^{-7}	2860×10^{-7}	First: ZAIRE	$24{,}915 \times 10^{-7}$	
					Top quarter: KORE.S	541×10^{-7}	

O60 FISH IMPORTS / GNP

1.87   3.74

Median:	VENEZU	192×10^{-7}
Bottom quarter:	SIERRA	35×10^{-7}
Last:	BAHAMA	2×10^{-7}
First:	HAITI	29.30
Top quarter:	SWITZD	1.99
Median:	POLAND	.63
Bottom quarter:	TUNISI	.02
Last:	MONGOL (28)	0

O61 FISH EXPORTS / GNP

4.99   23.85

First:	ICELAN	217.13
Top quarter:	MEXICO	1.83
Median:	ALGERI	.23
Bottom quarter:	HAITI (36)	0
Last:	LESOTH (36)	0

O62 OFFSHORE OIL PROD. / GNP

0.000536   0.003388

First:	QATAR	.031792
Top quarter:	ECUADR (125)	0

124

Table 3A-1—*Continued*

Variable Name	Units	Explanation	Mean	Standard Deviation	Examples Name	Value	Source
					Median: SPAIN (125)	0	
					Bottom quarter: TANZAN (125)	0	
					Last: SANMAR (125)	0	
063 U.N. LOS DELEGATION GNP			0.00938	0.02210	First: NAURU	.21429	
					Top quarter: NIGER	.00763	
					Median: URUGUA	.00268	
					Bottom quarter: PAKIST	.00080	
					Last: BURUND (7)	0	

4

Conclusions and Summary

Conclusions

The approach taken here makes it possible to characterize the marine policies of states according to objectively defined and rigorously applied national attributes. Rather than repeat information already explained, one additional application of the model is offered. Table 4-1 applies the information developed in the factor analysis of the data matrix containing all marine variables. These eight factors comprise the table:

Factor 2: Relative Coastal Marine Size
Factor 3: Zone Size and Claim
Factor 4: Geneva Conventions' Acceptance
Factor 5: Relative Research and Merchant Shipping Importance
Factor 6: Offshore Oil
Factor 7: Shipping-Fishing Importance
Factor 9: Marine Size-Wealth
Factor 10: Relative Flag Tonnage and Shipping Importance

In several instances where loadings are negative, the scores have been adjusted to avoid confusion.

Table 4-1 has simplified the factor score results by substituting high (H), medium (M), and low (L) for the actual factor scores. Low is defined as anything less than -.50, high as anything greater than +.50, and medium as anything in between. Even with this degree of simplification there is a bewildering array of possible country profiles. From the many country profiles, several patterns seem to emerge.

A group of Latin American countries have very similar profiles as defined in the table—they are Argentina, Brazil, Chile, Ecuador, El Salvador, Sierra Leone, and Uruguay. The set of characteristics that identifies this grouping is "low" values on factors 6, 7, and 9, corresponding to below-average offshore oil, shipping-fishing importance, and marine size-wealth. On most of the other factors this group's scores "medium" except for factor 3 (Zone Size-Claim) where they all score "high." Thus this pattern is unique to Latin America.

Most of the landlocked states seemed to have been identified by a particular pattern of factor scores consisting of low values of factor 3 (Zone Size-Claim) and factor 4 (Geneva Conventions' Acceptance). Nearly all these states have

Table 4-1
Country Marine Factor Score Characteristics

Country	Factor 2	Factor 3	Factor 4	Factor 5	Factor 6	Factor 7	Factor 9	Facto 10
Afghanistan	M	L	M	M	M	M	M	M
Albania	M	M	M	M	M	M	H	M
Algeria	M	L	M	M	M	M	M	M
Argentina	M	H	M	M	L	L	L	M
Australia	M	M	H	M	M	L	M	M
Austria	M	L	M	M	M	M	M	M
Bahamas	M	M	M	H	M	L	H	M
Bahrain	H	L	L	M	H	M	M	L
Bangladesh	M	H	L	H	M	L	M	M
Barbados	M	M	M	M	M	H	M	M
Belgium	M	L	H	M	M	M	L	M
Bolivia	M	L	M	M	M	M	M	M
Botswana	M	L	L	M	M	M	M	M
Brazil	M	H	L	M	L	L	L	M
Bulgaria	M	H	H	M	M	M	M	L
Burma	M	H	L	M	M	M	H	M
Burundi	M	L	L	M	M	M	M	M
Cambodia	M	H	H	M	M	M	M	M
Cameroon	M	H	M	M	M	M	M	M
Canada	M	M	M	M	L	M	M	M
Central African Republic	M	L	M	M	M	M	M	M
Chad	M	L	L	M	M	M	M	M
Chile	M	H	M	M	L	M	L	M
China	M	M	L	M	M	M	H	L
Colombia	M	H	H	M	M	L	M	M
Congo	M	M	L	M	M	M	M	M
Costa Rica	M	M	M	M	M	L	M	M
Cuba	M	M	M	M	M	M	M	M
Cyprus	M	M	M	M	M	M	M	M
Czechoslovakia	M	L	H	M	M	M	M	M
Dahomey	M	H	L	M	M	M	M	L
Denmark	M	L	H	M	M	H	M	M
Dominican Republic	M	L	H	M	M	M	M	M
Ecuador	M	H	L	M	L	L	L	M
El Salvador	M	H	L	M	L	L	L	M
Ethiopia	M	M	H	M	M	M	M	M
Fiji	M	M	H	M	M	M	M	M
Finland	M	H	H	M	M	M	M	M
France	M	M	M	M	M	M	M	M
Gabon	M	H	L	M	H	M	L	M
Gambia	H	M	L	M	M	M	M	M
Germany (E)	M	H	L	M	M	M	M	M
Germany (W)	M	L	M	M	M	M	M	M
Ghana	L	M	M	M	M	M	M	M
Greece	M	M	M	M	M	M	M	M

Country	Factor 2	Factor 3	Factor 4	Factor 5	Factor 6	Factor 7	Factor 9	Factor 10
atemala	M	M	H	M	M	M	M	M
inea	M	H	L	M	M	M	M	M
yana	M	M	L	M	M	M	M	M
iti	M	M	H	M	M	M	M	L
nduras	M	H	L	M	M	L	M	L
ngary	M	L	M	M	M	M	M	M
land	L	H	H	L	H	H	M	H
ia	M	M	L	M	L	M	M	M
onesia	M	H	M	M	M	L	H	M
n	M	M	M	M	H	M	M	M
q	M	L	L	M	M	L	M	M
land	M	H	M	M	M	M	M	M
ael	M	M	H	M	M	M	H	M
ly	M	L	M	M	M	M	L	M
ry Coast	M	M	L	M	M	M	L	M
naica	M	M	H	M	M	M	M	M
an	M	L	L	M	L	H	M	L
dan	M	L	L	M	M	M	M	M
nya	M	M	H	M	M	M	M	M
rea (N)	M	H	L	M	M	M	H	M
rea (S)	M	H	L	M	M	M	M	M
wait	M	M	M	M	H	M	M	M
s	M	L	L	M	M	M	M	M
anon	M	L	M	M	M	M	M	M
otho	M	L	L	M	L	M	M	M
eria	M	M	M	H	H	H	L	M
ya	M	M	M	M	H	M	M	L
chtenstein	M	L	L	M	M	M	M	M
xembourg	M	L	L	M	M	M	M	M
agasy Republic	M	M	H	M	M	M	L	M
awi	M	L	H	M	M	M	M	M
aysia	M	M	H	M	M	M	M	M
dive Islands	H	L	L	M	M	L	M	H
i	M	L	L	M	M	M	M	M
ta	H	M	H	M	L	M	M	L
uritania	M	H	M	M	H	M	M	M
uritius	H	H	H	M	M	M	M	L
xico	M	H	H	M	M	L	L	M
naco	H	L	L	M	M	L	L	H
ngolia	M	L	L	M	M	M	M	M
rocco	M	M	L	M	L	M	M	M
ru	H	M	L	M	M	M	M	L
al	M	L	M	M	M	M	M	M
herlands	M	H	H	M	M	H	M	M
w Zealand	M	M	H	M	M	M	M	M
aragua	M	M	L	M	L	M	M	M
er	M	L	L	M	M	M	M	M
eria	M	M	H	M	H	L	M	M
rway	M	H	M	H	M	H	M	M
an	M	M	L	M	H	M	M	M

Table 4-1 – *Continued*

Country	Factor 2	Factor 3	Factor 4	Factor 5	Factor 6	Factor 7	Factor 9	Fact 10
Pakistan	M	M	M	M	M	M	M	M
Panama	M	H	M	H	L	L	L	H
Paraguay	M	L	L	M	M	M	M	M
Peru	L	H	L	L	M	H	M	H
Philippines	M	H	L	M	L	L	L	H
Poland	M	L	M	M	M	M	M	M
Portugal	L	M	H	M	M	H	M	H
Qatar	M	M	L	M	H	M	M	M
Romania	M	M	H	M	M	M	M	M
Rwanda	M	L	L	M	M	M	M	M
San Marino	M	L	L	M	M	M	M	M
Saudi Arabia	L	M	L	M	H	L	L	M
Senegal	M	H	M	M	M	M	M	M
Sierra Leone	M	H	H	M	L	L	L	M
Singapore	M	M	M	M	M	M	M	M
Somalia	M	H	L	M	L	L	M	H
South Africa	M	M	H	M	M	M	M	M
Southern Yemen	M	H	L	M	H	H	H	M
Spain	M	H	H	M	M	H	M	M
Sri Lanka	M	H	M	M	M	M	M	M
Tanzania	M	M	L	M	M	M	M	M
Thailand	M	M	H	M	M	M	M	M
Togo	M	H	L	M	M	M	M	L
Tonga	H	M	H	M	L	M	M	L
Trinidad and Tobago	M	M	H	M	H	M	M	M
Tunisia	M	M	M	M	M	M	M	M
Turkey	M	H	M	M	M	M	H	L
Uganda	M	L	H	M	M	M	M	M
Uruguay	M	H	M	M	L	L	L	M
USSR	M	L	M	M	L	M	H	M
United Arab Republic	M	M	M	M	M	L	H	M
United Kingdom	M	M	H	H	M	M	M	M
United States of America	M	M	M	M	H	L	H	M
Upper Volta	M	L	M	M	L	M	M	M
Venezuela	M	M	H	M	M	M	M	M
Vietnam	M	H	L	M	M	M	H	M
Western Samoa	M	H	L	M	M	M	M	M
Yemen	M	M	L	M	M	M	M	M
Yugoslavia	M	L	H	M	M	H	M	M
Zaire	M	H	L	M	M	M	M	L
Zambia	M	L	L	M	M	M	M	M

medium scores on all the other factors. Countries involved in this group are Botswana, Burundi, Chad, Iraq, Jordan, Laos, Lesotho, Liechtenstein, Luxembourg, Mali, Mongolia, Niger, Paraguay, Rwanda, San Marino, and Zambia. In the few instances where a landlocked state was omitted from this group, for example, Hungary, it was due to its having some degree of acceptance of the 1958 Geneva Conventions.

A smaller group of states consisting of Bulgaria, Cambodia, Columbia, Mexico, and the Netherlands is typified by high scores on Zone Size-Claim and by Acceptance of the 1958 Geneva Conventions. Most of the rest of the scores for these countries fall in the medium category. It is a somewhat unlikely aggregation of states, not making as much intuitive sense as was the case in the first two groups.

It is interesting to see how the superpowers fare on this type of a formulation. The Soviet Union received medium scores on all but three of the factors. The Soviet scores on Zone Size-Claim and on Offshore Oil were all low. Only on factor 9, Marine Size-Wealth, does the Soviet Union have a high score. The United States has average scores on five of the eight factors. On Marine Size-Wealth and Offshore Oil the United States achieves high scores. Only on factor 7, Shipping-Fishing Importance does the United States place in the low category. In both instances, the scores would seem consistent with the real-world positions of these two states.

Next it is desirable to look at the five states examined in detail in chapter 2 to see how the results in table 4-1 correspond with the earlier findings. Canada achieved medium scores on all but Offshore Oil on which she had a score of low. These results are somewhat perplexing. Canada's huge continental shelf and coastline surely contributed to a high score on factor 3, but this was probably offset by her modest claim to territorial sea and exclusive fisheries zone. It also seems likely that many important environmental concerns may not have been reflected in the factor scores. China has all scores in the medium category with the exception of low values on Acceptance of the 1958 Geneva Conventions and Relative Flag Tonnage and Shipping Importance and, of course, a high value on Marine Size-Wealth. These findings are completely consistent with the picture painted of China. Her huge size means that the relativistic variables seldom achieve high scores.

Iran also scored about as would be expected. Iran's scores are all in the medium range except for Offshore Oil, on which her petroleum dominance is in evidence. These results are consistent except that the recent naval build-up has yet to be reflected in the factor scores. All of Nigeria's scores are medium except for three. There are highs on Acceptance of the 1958 Geneva Conventions and Offshore Oil, a low on Fishing-Shipping Importance. Again these results are consistent with the earlier discussion of the Nigerian situation. The scores achieved for the Philippines are somewhat surprising. One finds high scores on Zone Size-Claim and on Relative Flag Tonnage, but low scores on Acceptance of the 1958 Geneva Conventions, Offshore Oil, Shipping-Fishing Importance, and Marine Size-Wealth. Two things are clear here. First, the factor scores place the Philippines very clearly in a less-developed country category.

Second, the model may not be sensitive enough to the characteristics of archipelagic states.

On balance, however, the scores contain few surprises, that is, the macroscopic techniques seem to have provided much of the same information obtained from detailed examination of individual countries. It is encouraging that Iceland has the greatest number of high scores, five from a total of eight. Iceland has high scores on Zone Size-Claim, Acceptance of the 1958 Geneva Conventions, Offshore Oil, Shipping-Fishing Importance and Relative Flag Tonnage-Shipping Importance. Since the complete dependence of Iceland on the ocean is well documented, results like this are to be expected.

Summary

There can be little doubt that the analyses of marine policy presented here have been broadly comparative. It has been forecast that comparative analyses of policy will rapidly expand in the future and occupy an increasing amount of academic attention.[1] Whether this will be the case with marine policy remains to be seen. In any event, the working premise here has been that a truly comparative approach to marine policy is necessary and desirable. Marine policy has been defined as a set of goals, directives, and intentions formulated by authoritative persons and having some relation to the marine environment. This was a sufficiently broad definition to permit the model to include many different kinds of national characteristics.

The approach adopted to examine marine policy was a reflection of a problem inherent in researching such a subject. One has to make an important decision about how much relative emphasis to place on breadth or depth of analysis. The examination of five specific states' marine policies before adopting a macroscopic approach was an attempt to accommodate both strategies. Generally it was found that the two approaches complemented each other. The great data-reduction capabilities of factor analysis did not obscure most of the individual idiosyncrasies of countries.

Table 4-1 should demonstrate conclusively that it is futile to try to force the countries of the world into a few simple categories and expect them to behave in "appropriate" ways. Even with considerable oversimplification in the table, there are still over 2,000 possible country marine profiles. As the Third United Nations Law of the Sea Conference nears some sort of a climax, it is imperative that we have systematic information about state relationships to the marine environment. This study has provided such information. It is hoped that the patterns of behavior uncovered here will help to illuminate and explain the complicated set of national actions that will occur in the next decade, a decade that will see global acceptance of 200-mile economic zones, commercial exploitation of manganese nodules, and the assertion of unprecedented claims and counterclaims to hydrospace.

Appendix A

Three-Letter Country
Abbreviations

AFG	Kingdom of Afghanistan
ALB	People's Republic of Albania
ALG	Democratic and Popular Republic of Algeria
ARG	Argentine Republic
AUL	Commonwealth of Australia
AUS	Republic of Austria
BAM	The Bahamas
BAH	Bahrain
BAN	Bangladesh
BAR	Barbados
BEL	Kingdom of Belgium
BOL	Republic of Bolivia
BOT	Botswana
BRA	Federative Republic of Brazil
BUL	People's Republic of Bulgaria
BUA	Union of Burma
BUI	Republic of Burundi
CAB	Kingdom of Cambodia
CAM	Federal Republic of Cameroon
CAN	Canada
CAR	Central Africa Republic
CHA	Republic of Chad
CHE	Republic of Chile
CHN	People's Republic of China
COL	Republic of Colombia
CON	People's Republic of Congo
COS	Republic of Costa Rica
CUB	Republic of Cuba
CYP	Republic of Cyprus
CZE	Czechoslovak Socialist Republic
DAH	Republic of Dahomey
DEN	Kingdom of Denmark
DOM	Dominican Republic
ECU	Republic of Ecuador
ELS	Republic of El Salvador
ETH	Empire of Ethiopia
FIJ	Fiji

FIN	Republic of Finland
FRA	French Republic
GAB	Gabonese Republic
GAM	The Gambia
GEE	German Democratic Republic
GEW	Federal Republic of Germany
GHA	Republic of Ghana
GRE	Kingdom of Greece
GUA	Republic of Guatemala
GUI	Republic of Guinea
GUY	Republic of Guyana
HAI	Republic of Haiti
HON	Republic of Honduras
HUN	Hungarian People's Republic
ICE	Republic of Iceland
INA	Republic of India
INS	Republic of Indonesia
IRN	Iran
IRQ	Republic of Iraq
IRE	Republic of Ireland
ISR	State of Israel
ITA	Republic of Italy
IVO	Republic of Ivory Coast
JAM	Jamaica
JAP	Japan
JOR	Hashemite Kingdom of Jordan
KEN	Republic of Kenya
KON	Democratic People's Republic of Korea
KOS	Republic of Korea
KUW	State of Kuwait
LAO	Kingdom of Laos
LEB	Republic of Lebanon
LES	Kingdom of Lesotho
LIB	Republic of Liberia
LIY	Libyan Arab Republic
LIE	Principality of Liechtenstein
LUX	Grand Duchy of Luxembourg
MAY	Malagasy Republic
MAI	Republic of Malawi
MAA	Malaysia
MAD	Maldive Islands
MAR	Mali Republic
MAL	Malta

MAU	Islamic Republic of Mauritania
MAS	United Mexican States
MOO	Principality of Monaco
MOA	Mongolian People's Republic
MOR	Kingdom of Morocco
NAU	Republic of Nauru
NEP	Nepal
NET	Kingdom of the Netherlands
NEW	New Zealand
NIC	Republic of Nicaragua
NIR	Republic of the Niger
NIA	Federal Republic of Nigeria
NOR	Kingdom of Norway
OMA	Sultanate of Oman
PAK	Islamic Republic of Pakistan
PAN	Republic of Panama
PAR	Republic of Paraguay
PER	Republic of Peru
PHI	Republic of the Philippines
POL	Polish People's Republic
POR	Portuguese Republic
QAT	Qatar
ROM	Socialist Republic of Romania
RWA	Republic of Rwanda
SAN	Republic of San Marino
SAU	Kingdom of Saudi Arabia
SEN	Republic of Senegal
SIE	Sierra Leone
SIN	Republic of Singapore
SOM	Somali Democratic Republic
SAF	Republic of South Africa
SYE	People's Republic of Southern Yemen
SPA	The Spanish State
SRL	Sri Lanka
SUD	Republic of the Sudan
SWA	Kingdom of Swaziland
SWE	Kingdom of Sweden
SWI	Switzerland
SYR	Syrian Arab Republic
TAN	United Republic of Tanzania
THA	Thailand
TOG	Republic of Togo
TON	Kingdom of Tonga

TRI	Trinidad and Tobago
TUN	Republic of Tunisia
TUR	Republic of Turkey
UGA	Republic of Uganda
URU	Eastern Republic of Uruguay
USR	Union of Soviet Socialist Republics
UAR	United Arab Republic
UK	United Kingdom of Great Britain and Northern Ireland
USA	United States of America
UPV	Republic of Upper Volta
VEN	Republic of Venezuela
VNN	Democratic Republic of Vietnam
VNS	Republic of Vietnam
WSA	Independent State of Western Samoa
YEM	Yemen Arab Republic
YUG	Socialist Federal Republic of Yugoslavia
ZAI	Republic of Zaire
ZAM	Republic of Zambia

Notes

Notes

Chapter 1

Introduction

1. William Wallace, *The Logic of Hegel* (London: Oxford University Press, 1931), p. 204.

2. Charles C. Bates and Paul Yost, "Where Trends the Flow of Merchant Ships?" in John King Gamble, Jr. and Giulio Pontecorvo (eds.), *Law of the Sea: The Emerging Regime of the Oceans* (Cambridge: Ballinger Publishing Company, 1974), p. 257.

3. F.E. Popper, "The Role of FAO and of the Regional Organizations after the Conclusion of the Third United Nations Conference on the Law of the Sea," in Francis T. Christy, Jr.; Thomas A. Clingan, Jr.; John King Gamble, Jr.; H. Gary Knight; and Edward Miles (eds.), *Law of the Sea: Caracas and Beyond* (Cambridge: Ballinger Publishing Company, 1974), p. 211.

4. John P. Albers, "Offshore Petroleum: Its Geography and Technology," in Gamble and Pontecorvo (eds.), *Law of the Sea: The Emerging Regime of the Oceans,* p. 294.

5. Ibid., p. 303.

6. Jon L. Jacobson and Thomas A. Hanlon, "Regulation of Hard-Mineral Mining on the Continental Shelf," *Oregon Law Review* L (1971), 426.

7. Kanenas, "Wide Limits and 'Equitable' Distribution of Seabed Resources," *Ocean Development and International Law* I, No. 2 (1973), 144.

8. Richard I. Hofferbert, *The Study of Public Policy* (New York: Bobbs-Merrill, 1974), p. 4.

9. Ibid., p. 5.

10. Heinz Eulau and Robert Eyestone, "Policy Maps of City Councils and Policy Outcomes: A Developmental Analysis," *American Political Science Review* LXII (March 1968), 126.

11. Philip M. Gregg (ed.), *Problems of Theory in Policy Analysis* (Lexington: Lexington Books, D.C. Heath and Company, 1976), p. 152.

12. Ibid., p. 157.

13. Bernard C. Cohen and Scott A. Harris, "Foreign Policy," in Fred I. Greenstein and Nelson W. Polsby (eds.), *Handbook of Political Science* (Reading, Mass.: Addison-Wesley Publishing Company, 1975), VI, p. 383.

14. Hofferbert, *Study of Public Policy,* p. 259.

15. Gregg, *Problems in Policy Analysis,* p. 154.

16. Ibid., p. 63.

17. Ibid., p. 64.

18. John G. Grumm, "The Analysis of Policy Impact," in Greenstein and Polsby (eds.), *Handbook,* p. 441.

19. Eulau and Eyestone, *Policy Maps,* p. 126.

20. Cohen and Harris, "Foreign Policy," pp. 382–383.

21. David Easton, *A Systems Analysis of Political Life* (New York: John Wiley and Sons, 1965), p. 351.

22. Ibid.

23. Robert L. Friedheim and Judith T. Kildow, *Report on the Ocean Policy Research Workshop,* Occasional Paper #26 (Kingston, R.I.: Law of the Sea Institute, 1975), p. 3.

24. Barry G. Buzan and Barbara Johnson, *Canada at the Third Law of the Sea Conference: Policy, Role and Prospects,* Occasional Paper #29 (Kingston, R.I.: Law of the Sea Institute, 1975), p. 10.

25. E.D. Brown, "Our Nation and the Sea: A Comment on the Proposed Legal-Political Framework for the Development of Submarine Mineral Resources," in Lewis M. Alexander (ed.), *The Law of the Sea: National Policy Recommendations* (Kingston, R.I.: University of Rhode Island, 1970), pp. 25–27.

26. Kenneth H. Kolb, "Congress and the Ocean Policy Process," *Ocean Development and International Law* III, No. 3 (1976), 263.

27. Ann L. Hollick and Robert E. Osgood, *New Era of Ocean Politics* (Baltimore: Johns Hopkins University Press, 1974), p. 1.

28. Myres S. McDougal and William T. Burke, *The Public Order of the Oceans* (New Haven: Yale University Press, 1962), p. ix.

29. Norman J. Padelford, *Public Policy and the Uses of the Seas* (Cambridge: Massachusetts Institute of Technology, 1968), p. 6.

30. Kolb, "Congress and Ocean Policy," p. 262.

31. J.S. Nye, "Ocean Rule Making from a World Politics Perspective," *Ocean Development and International Law* III, No. 1 (1975), 31.

32. Hollick and Osgood, *New Era,* p. 75.

33. Davis B. Bobrow, "International Politics and High-Level Decision Making: Context for Ocean Policy," *ODIL* III, No. 2 (1975), 172.

34. Ibid.

35. Friedheim and Kildow, *Report on Ocean Policy,* p. 9.

36. Buzan and Johnson, *Canada,* p. 10

Chapter 2

Marine Police: Five Specific Cases

1. R. Gordon Robertson, "The Long Gaze," in Irving N. Smith et al. (eds.), *The Unbelievable Land* (Department of Northern Affairs and Natural Resources and the Northern Service of CBC, 1964), p. 134.

2. George Grant, *Lament for a Nation* (Princeton: D. Van Nostrand, 1965), recurring theme throughout book.

3. Ronald S. Ritchie, "Canada's Institute for Research on Public Policy," *The Canadian Business Review* I, No. 1 (1974), 41.

4. G. Bruce Doern and Peter Aucoin, *The Structures of Policy Making in Canada* (Toronto: Bryant, 1971), p. 27.

5. Ann L. Hollick, "United States and Canadian Policy Processes in Law of the Sea," *San Diego Law Review* XII (1975), 537.

6. Ibid.

7. Arthur H. Dean, "The Geneva Conference on the Law of the Sea," *American Journal of International Law* LII (1958), 612.

8. Ibid., p. 614.

9. Arthur H. Dean, "The Second Geneva Conference on the Law of the Sea," *American Journal of International Law* LIV (1960), 774.

10. *Commons Debates* (Canada House of Commons [Ottawa, 15 May 1969]), p. 8720.

11. *Commons Debates* (Canada House of Commons [Ottawa, 17 April 1970]), p. 6029.

12. Barry G. Buzan and Barbara Johnson, *Canada at the Third Law of the Sea Conference: Policy, Role and Prospects,* Occasional Paper #29 (Kingston, R.I.: Law of the Sea Institute, 1975), p. 6.

13. Ibid.

14. Hollick, "United States and Canadian Policy," pp. 539-541.

15. *Commons Debates* (Canada House of Commons [Ottawa, 17 April 1970]), p. 5950.

16. *The People's Republic of China: An Economic Assessment* (U.S. Congress, Joint Economic Committee [Washington, D.C.: U.S. Government Printing Office, 1972]), p. 178.

17. A. Doak Barnett, *Uncertain Passage: China's Transition to the Post Mao Era* (Washington, D.C.: Brookings Institution, 1974), p. 165.

18. U.S. Congress, *The People's Republic of China,* p. 168.

19. C.P. Fitzgerald, *The Chinese View of Their Place in the World* (London: Oxford University Press, 1964), pp. 26-32.

20. Barnett, *Uncertain Passage,* pp. 19-20. Fitzgerald, *Chinese View,* pp. 68-72.

21. Fitzgerald, *Chinese View,* p. 1-72.

22. J.K. Holloway, Jr., "The Red Navy's Role in the Sino-Soviet Split," *U.S. Naval Institute Proceedings* (September 1973), 18-24.

23. *The Military Balance 1974-1975* (The International Institute for Strategic Studies [London, 1974]), pp. 48-50.

24. *Communist China: A Bibliographic Survey* (U.S. Department of Army Headquarters [Washington, D.C.: U.S. Government Printing Office, 1971]), pp. 104-105.

25. A Doak Barnett, *A New U.S. Policy Toward China* (Washington, D.C.: Brookings Institution, 1971), pp. 43-45 and 129-133.

26. Barnett, *Uncertain Passage,* pp. 2-3.

27. Fitzgerald, *Chinese View,* pp. 56-72.

28. Barnett, *Uncertain Passage,* pp. 1-66 and 245-250.

29. U.S. Congress, *The People's Republic of China,* p. 14.

30. Choon-Ho Park, *Continental Shelf Issues in the Yellow Sea and the East China Sea,* Occasional Paper #15 (Kingston, R.I.: Law of the Sea Institute, 1972), pp. 2-4 and 23-26; "Building Railroads on the Sea: China's Attitude Toward Maritime Law," *The China Quarterly* (July-September 1974) 550-553.

31. Barnett, *Uncertain Passage,* pp. 136-154.

32. Ibid.

33. Park, "Building Railroads," pp. 553-554.

34. Ibid.

35. Ibid., pp. 552-554; Park, *Continental Shelf Issues,* pp. 25-26.

36. Park, "Building Railroads," pp. 552-554.

37. United Nations *Economic Bulletin for Asia and the Far East* Vol. XXIV, No. 1 [New York, June 1973]), p. 46.

38. *Yearbook of Fisheries Statistics 1973* (United Nations, Food and Agricultural Organization [Rome, 1974]), pp. 52 and 96; Choon-Ho Park, "Fishing In Troubled Waters: The Northeast Asia Fisheries Controversy," *Ocean Development and International Law* II, No. 2 (1974), 127-128 and 96-98.

39. Park, "Fishing in Troubled Waters," pp. 23-26.

40. *Statistical Tables for 1974* (Lloyd's Register of Shipping [London, 1974]); *U.N. Statistical Yearbook 1973* (United Nations Statistical Office [New York, 1974]), p. 442; *Communist China 1970* (Union Research Institute [Hong Kong, 1971]), pp. 248-253; U.S. Congress, *The People's Republic of China,* pp. 148-178.

41. Ibid., p. 14.

42. Ibid.

43. Thomas W. Robinson, "China in 1973: Renewed Leftism Threatens the 'New Course,' " *Asian Survey* XIV, No. 1 (1974), 1-21; Barnett, *Uncertain Passage,* pp. 163-167, 360.

44. Lloyd's, *Statistical Tables,* p. 442.

45. Ibid.

46. Union Research Institute, *Communist China 1970,* pp. 248-253; Park, "Building Railroads," pp. 554-555.

47. Barnett, *Uncertain Passage,* pp. 284-295; "Quarterly Chronicle and Documentation, January-March," *The China Quarterly,* No. 58 (May 1974), 405.

48. Ibid.

49. John E. Moore (ed.), *Janes Fighting Ships 1974-1975* (London: Janes Yearbooks, 1974), pp. 76-83; Barnett, *Uncertain Passage,* pp. 295-296.

50. Park, "Building Railroads," pp. 548-550.

51. Moore, *Janes,* pp. 76-83; 642-643.

52. U.S. Congress, *The People's Republic of China,* pp. 11-12. International Institute, *Military Balance,* pp. 48-50.

53. Park, "Building Railroads," pp. 544-545.

54. Ibid., pp. 544-550; Robin Churchill, K.R. Simmonds, and Jane Welch, *New Directions in the Law of the Sea: Collected Papers* (Dobbs Ferry, N.Y.: Oceana Publications, Inc., 1973), III, pp. 318-320.

55. Park, "Building Railroads," pp. 544-547.

56. Ibid., pp. 544-557; Churchill et al., *New Directions,* pp. 178, 318-320.

57. Park, "Fishing in Troubled Waters," pp. 110-126; Park, "Building Railroads," pp. 544-557.

58. Park, "Building Railroads," pp. 544-547.

59. Park, "Fishing in Troubled Waters," pp. 110-126.

60. U.S. Congress, *The People's Republic of China,* p. 14; *The Long-Range Future of the Navy* (U.S. Naval War College, unpublished Group Research Project Report [Newport, R.I., 1972]), pp. 1-31.

61. *Statistical Yearbook, 1975,* (New York: United Nations, 1976), p. 191.

62. James F. Clarity, "The Shah Seeks to Regain the Glories of Darius," *The Providence Sunday Journal,* December 15, 1974, p. F-13.

63. Leon Seltzer (ed.), *The Columbian Lippincott Gazetteer of the World* (New York: Columbia University Press, 1952), p. 844.

64. Rouhollah K. Ramazani, *The Northern Tier: Afghanistan, Iran and Turkey* (Princeton: D. Van Nostrand, 1966), p. 77.

142

65. *Quarterly Economic Review* (Economist Intelligence Unit Ltd., Iran No. 1–1974 [London, 1974]), p. 12.

66. *Fishery Country Profile* (United Nations, Food and Agriculture Organization of the U.N., FID/CP/IRA [1970]).

67. Ibid.

68. W.H. Keddie, "Fish and Futility in Iranian Development," *Journal of Developing Areas* (October 1971), 26.

69. John Marlowe, *Iran* (New York: Praeger, 1963), pp. 3–10.

70. James A. Bill, "The Plasticity of Informal Politics: the Case of Iran," *Middle East Journal* (Spring 1973), 144.

71. James A. Bill, *The Politics of Iran: Groups, Classes and Modernization* (Columbus, Ohio: Charles E. Merrill, 1972), p. 153.

72. Economist Intelligence Unit, *Quarterly Economic Review* (1973) (all economic statistics from Iranian sources).

73. Rouhalla K. Ramazani, *The Persian Gulf: Iran's Role* (Charlottesville, Va: University Press of Virginia, 1972), p. 71.

74. *National Claims to Maritime Jurisdiction,* Limits in the Seas, No. 36 (U.S. Department of State, Office of the Geographer Washington, D.C., [revised April 1, 1974]), p. 54.

75. United Nations Document A/CONF .62/C.2/L.27, July 29, 1974.

76. United Nations Document A/CONF .62/SR.23 (Vol. I, *Official Record of Third U.N. Conference on Law of the Sea*), 1975, p. 71.

77. Ibid., p. 72.

78. Ibid.

79. United Nations Document ST/LEG/SER.B/18, 1974, pp. 99–100.

80. United Nations Document A/CONF.62/C.3/SR.6, pp. 3–4.

81. United Nations Document A/CONF.62/C.2/SR.43, pp. 9–10.

82. Arnaud de Borchgrave, "Colossus of the Oil Lanes," *Newsweek* (May 21, 1973), 40.

83. Ibid., p. 41.

84. Ibid.

85. Ibid.

86. *The Washington Post,* March 23, 1973, p. A-1.

87. Robert E. Osgood, "U.S. Security Interests in Ocean Law," *ODIL* II, No. 1 (1974), 27.

88. William Graves, "Iran: Desert Miracle," *National Geographic* CXLVII, No. 1 (January 1975), 35.

89. Suzanne Cronje, *The World and Nigeria* (London: Sidgwick and Jackson, 1972), p. 10.

90. John M. Ostheimer, *Nigerian Politics* (New York: Harper and Row, 1973), p. 37.

91. Joseph Okpaku (ed.), *Nigeria: Dilemma of Nationhood* (New York: Third Press, 1972), p. 367.

92. "Nigeria: Exit Gowon," *Africa* XLIX (September 1975), 10.

93. Ibid.

94. *New York Times,* February 22, 1976.

95. Alan Rake, "Olusegun Obasanjo—New Man at the Top," *African Development* X (April 1976), 431.

96. Robert W. Brown, "Africa's Giant Oilfields," *Africa Report* (March-April 1975), 50.

97. John Hatch, *Nigeria: A History* (London: Secker and Warburg, 1971), p. 255.

98. *New York Times,* August 10, 1975.

99. David J. Murray, "The Federation of Nigeria," *Current History* LX (March 1971), 159-160.

100. Harold D. Nelson et al., *Area Handbook for Nigeria* (Washington, D.C.: U.S. Government Printing Office, 1972), p. 241.

101. Hatch, *Nigeria,* p. 263.

102. Hatch, *Nigeria,* p. 255.

103. Nelson et al., *Area Handbook,* pp. 243-245.

104. Ralph Uwechve, "Lt. General Obasanjo," *Africa* LVIII, No. 58 (June 1976), 10.

105. Ibid., p. 12.

106. Rake, "Olusegun Obasanjo—New Man," p. 431.

107. Guy Arnold, "Nigeria: The First Seven Months," *African Development* X (March 1976), 223.

108. Nelson et al., *Area Handbook,* p. 346.

109. Arthur O. Ezenekwe, "Nigeria Develops Fishing to Meet Food Demand," *Fishing News International* (September 1974), 47.

110. Ezenekwe, "Nigeria Develops Fishing," p. 46.

111. G.E. Emembolu and S.S. Pannu, "Africa: Oil and Development," *Africa Today* XXII (October-December, 1975), 44-45.

112. Brown, "Giant Oilfields," p. 51.

113. *New York Times,* October 2, 1974, p. 4:4.

114. Nelson et al., *Area Handbook,* pp. 238-249.

115. Nelson et al., *Area Handbook,* p. 251.

116. Nelson et al., *Area Handbook,* p. 260.

117. Oye Ogunbadejo, "Nigeria and the Great Powers," *African Affairs* LXXV (January 1976), 14-17.

118. Nelson et al., *Area Handbook,* p. 346.

119. Nelson et al., *Area Handbook,* p. 353.

120. John Oyinbo, *Nigeria: Crisis and Beyond* (London: Charles Knight, 1971), pp. 134-138.

121. Ibid., p. xxii

122. *Background Notes: The Philippines* (U.S. Department of State, Office of Media Services [Washington, D.C.: U.S. Government Printing Office, 1974]), p. 1.

123. Ibid.

124. Robert E. Huke, *Shadows on the Land: An Economic Geography of the Philippines* (Makati, Rizal, the Philippines: Carmelo and Bauermann, Inc., 1963), p. 370.

125. *Theoretical and Real Allocations of Seabed to Coastal States Based on Certain U.N. Seabeds Committee Proposals* (U.S. Department of State, The Geographer, International Boundary Study, Series A, Limits in the Seas #36 [Washington, D.C.: U.S. Government Printing Office, 1974]), p. 12.

126. Frederick H. Chaffee et al., *Area Handbook for the Philippines* (Washington, D.C.: U.S. Government Printing Office, 1969), p. 26.

127. Ibid.

128. U.S. Department of State, *Background Notes,* p. 4.

129. Beth Day, *The Philippines: Shattered Showcase of Democracy in Asia* (New York: M. Evans and Co., Inc., 1974), p. 57.

130. Ibid., p. 67.

131. Chaffee et al., *Area Handbook,* p. 5.

132. Bernardino Ronquillo, "Marcos Moves In," *Far Eastern Economic Review* XXCVII, No. 9 (February 28, 1975), 33.

133. Ibid.

134. Ibid.

135. Day, *The Philippines,* p. 43.

136. "Cotabato: Marcos' Offensive," *Far Eastern Economic Review* XXCVII, No. 8 (February 21, 1975), 11-12.

137. F.J. Doucet et al., *Institutional and Legal Aspects Affecting Fishery Development in Selected Countries Bordering the South China Sea,* F.A.O., U.N. Development Programme, Indo-Pacific Fisheries Council (Rome, 1973), p. 15.

138. Ibid.

139. Tadashi Yamamoto, *Review of Marine Fishery Statistical Systems in Countries Bordering the South China Sea and Proposals for Their Improvement*, F.A.O., U.N. Development Programme, Indo-Pacific Fisheries Council (Rome, 1973), 19.

140. Doucet et al., *Institutional and Legal Aspects*, p. 15.

141. Ibid.

142. Day, *The Philippines*, p. 41.

143. Ibid.

144. Doucet et al., *Institutional and Legal Aspects*, p. 19.

145. Ibid.

146. Ibid.

147. Joseph W. Dellapenna, "The Philippines' Territorial Water Claim in International Law," *Journal of Law and Economic Development* V (1970), 47.

148. Ibid., p. 46.

149. Leo J. Bouchez, *The Regime of Bays in International Law* (Leyden, Netherlands: A.W. Sythoff, 1964), p. 98.

150. Ibid.

151. Maureen Khin Thitsa Franssen, "The Archipelagic Principle," *Oceanus* XVII (1973), 15.

152. Ibid., p. 17.

153. Ibid.

154. *Report of the Committee on the Peaceful Uses of the Seabed and the Ocean Floor Beyond the Limits of National Jurisdiction* (General Assembly of the United Nations, Vol. III [New York, 1973]), p. 102.

155. Ibid., p. 104.

156. Dellapenna, "The Philippines' Claim," p. 51.

Chapter 3

General Application of the Model

1. John King Gamble, Jr., *Global Marine Attributes* (Cambridge: Ballinger Publishing Company, 1974).

2. Joseph M. Firestone, *Concept Formation, Systems Analysis and Factor Analysis in Political Science*, Dimensionality of Nations Project Research Report No. 23 (Honolulu: University of Hawaii, Department of Political Science, May, 1969), p. 7.

3. R.J. Rummel, "Understanding Factor Analysis," *Journal of Conflict Resolution* XI, No. 4 (December 1967), 445.

4. Lee F. Anderson, Meredith Watts, and Allen R. Wilcox, *Legislative Roll-Call Analysis* (Evanston, Illinois: Northwestern University Press, 1966), p. 127.

5. K.G. Joreskog, *Statistical Estimation in Factor Analysis* (Uppsala, Sweden: Almquist and Wiksell, 1963), p. 9.

6. Jack Block, "The Difference Between R and Q," *Psychological Review* LXII (1955), 356–358.

7. Rummel, "Understanding Factor Analysis," p. 477.

8. Gary Oliva and R.J. Rummel, *Foreign Conflict Patterns and Types for 1963,* Dimensionality of Nations Project Research Report No. 22, (Honolulu: University of Hawaii, Department of Political Science, 1969), p. 13.

9. R.J. Rummel, "Some Empirical Findings on Nations and Their Behavior," *World Politics* XXI, No. 2 (January 1969), 226–241; Arthur S. Banks and Robert E. Textor, *A Cross-Polity Survey* (Cambridge: The M.I.T. Press, 1963); Arthur S. Banks and Philip M. Gregg, "Grouping Political Systems: Q Factor Analysis of a Cross-Polity Survey," *American Behavioral Scientist* IX, No. 3 (November 1965), 5; Jack Sawyer, "Dimensions of Nations: Size, Wealth and Politics," *American Journal of Sociology* LXXIII, No. 2 (September 1967), 159.

Chapter 4

Conclusions and Summary

1. Richard I. Hofferbert, *The Study of Public Policy* (New York: Bobbs-Merrill, 1974), p. 269.

About the Author

John King Gamble, Jr. received the B.A. from the College of Wooster (Ohio) and the Ph.D. from the University of Washington. From 1971 until 1976, he was assistant professor of marine affairs and executive director of the Law of the Sea Institute at the University of Rhode Island. Currently, he is associate professor of political science and head of the Division of Social and Behavioral Sciences at The Behrend College, The Pennsylvania State University. Gamble's major academic interests are international law, marine affairs and marine policy, law of the sea, and social science methodologies. Other books by Gamble include *Global Marine Attributes, Law of the Sea: The Emerging Regime of the Oceans* and *The International Court of Justice: An Analysis of a Failure.*